Using Learning Contracts in Higher Education

Using Learning Contracts in Higher Education

EDITED BY

John Stephenson

and Michael Laycock

Routledge
Taylor & Francis Group
LONDON AND NEW YORK

First published in 1993 by Routledge
2 Park Square, Milton Park, Abingdon, Oxfordshire OX14 4RN
711 Third Avenue, New York, NY 10017

First issued in hardback 2017

Routledge is an imprint of the Taylor and Francis Group, an informa business

British Library Cataloguing in Publication Data

A CIP record for this book is available from the British Library.

ISBN 13: 978-1-138-16335-5 (hbk)
ISBN 13: 978-0-7494-0954-8 (pbk)

Typeset by Saxon Graphics Ltd, Derby

Contents

Acknowledgements

The authors have received a great deal of assistance in the preparation of this book, both in the organisation of the conference, 'Using Learning Contracts in Higher Education', of which the book represents the proceedings, and in the construction of the book itself. Considerable thanks are given to the following.

The RSA Higher Education for Capability project and particularly Helen Pearson and Naomi Wilds.

The sponsors of the conference: Enterprise in Higher Education and Digital Equipment Company Ltd.

The Enterprise Learning Programme of the University of East London and particularly Brenda Keer.

Ann Bailey, Digital Equipment Company Ltd, for chairing the conference.

The many colleagues who submitted articles for publication, in particular Elizabeth J Barnes, Adrian Evans, Della Fazey, John Fazey, Gerald McElwee and Ray Wallace.

The RSA for hosting the conference.

The Contributors

Ray Binns is Subject Leader in Maths/Stats in the School of Computing and IT, Principal Lecturer in Statistics, Course Leader for Enterprise in Information Technology.

Anne Brockbank, formerly Anne O'Connor of Manchester Polytechnic, is now a Senior Lecturer at the University of North London Business School. Anne specialises in the Behavioural Sciences, particularly skill development for students, working managers and mentors. She is currently co-authoring with Ian McGill, *Manager as Mentor* due to be published in 1993.

Don Currie is the Southern Water Fellow in Human Resource Management at the Southampton Institute Management Centre. He first developed learning contracts in 1984 with students on the Institute of Personnel Management course which he ran for 11 years. Mr Currie is an Applied Occupational Psychologist who worked in industry for 23 years.

Sue Drew is Senior Lecturer for the Personal Skills and Qualities Project at Sheffield Hallam University.

David Gosling is Coordinator for the Teaching and Learning Methods Unit and Philosophy Lecturer in the School of the Arts at Staffordshire University.

Sheila Harri-Augstein is joint head, with Laurie Thomas, of the post-graduate division of the Centre for the Study of Human Learning at Brunel University. As well as holding previous posts at the Open University and Loughborough University of Technology she is also a Zen master of Ikebana.

Christopher Harris is a member of a cross-Faculty unit within Anglia Polytechnic University responsible for the innovative further exploitation of credit-based learning. In addition to work with Learning Agreements his responsibilities include company accreditation, and issues of national and international credit-transfer.

Jean Hay-Smith is Clinical Supervisor for the University of East London and The Royal London Hospital and Associated Community Services Trust. Her main responsibilities are the supervision of the 4 Year BSc (Hons) Physiotherapy degree based at UEL and liaison with clinical physiotherapists providing practice placements.

Julie Hinchliffe is currently Programme Director for the Diploma in Management Studies at Bradford and Ilkley Community College. She has been much involved in key leadership roles and new initiatives in curriculum development.

Isabell Hodgson is Senior Lecturer in Food and Facilities Management at

Leeds Metropolitan University. Her prime responsibility is as Industrial Placement Coordinator for Hospitality Management Studies and other related courses. Between 200 and 250 places are to be located including overseas opportunities.

Tom Jones is Director of Negotiated Study in Birmingham Institute of Art and Design at the University of Central England and is currently undertaking research concerned with adult learning through practice of the visual arts.

Steve Lawson is a Senior Lecturer in Strategic Management and Course Leader of the Certificate in Management at Sheffield Business School, Sheffield Hallam University.

Mike Laycock is Programme Director of the Enterprise Learning Programme at the University of East London.

Iain Marshall is Director of Work-Based Learning at Napier University in Edinburgh.

Penny Marrington is Senior Lecturer in Business and Management. Her chapter arises from work in partnership with Richard Boyce. Both are founder members of the Management Development Programme course team at Sunderland Business School.

Mac McCarthy is Head of Organisation and Management Studies at Edge Hill College of Higher Education.

Margaret Mill is Project Assistant at Napier University within the Educational Development Unit.

Kathy Moore is Assistant Director at Roffey Park Management College, with a special interest in self-managed learning programmes.

David Nicholls is Head of the School of History at Manchester Metropolitan University where he has developed enterprise-related undergraduate courses.

Dave O'Reilly is Head of the Coordinating Unit for Independent Study at the University of East London. At the moment he is particularly involved in developing flexible course delivery systems.

John Piper has contributed to the Degree by Independent Study and also has institutional responsibility for quality assurance and modular courses at Crewe and Alsager Faculty, Manchester Metropolitan University.

Clive Robertson is Chair of Oxford Brookes University's CATS Committee and is responsible for Academic Quality Assurance in the Faculty of Business, Languages and Hotel Management. He has experience of the implementation of learning contracts in the work-place for employees and in Supervised Work Experience as well as within undergraduate programmes of study in the University. He also has experience of the accreditation of in-company training programmes.

Graham Spaull is currently Manager for Young People Development at Rover Group. He has experience of using learning agreements with students in summer placements, to provide a focus for the student and line manager as well as creating feedback for the student's higher education establishment.

John Stephenson has been Director of the RSA's Higher Education for Capability project since September 1988. He was head of the School for

Independent Study at North East London Polytechnic (now the University of East London) from 1978 to 1988.

Wendy Stewart-David is a Senior Lecturer in Human Resources Management and Development and a member of the Institute of Personnel Management. She is Deputy Course Leader of BA Business Studies and has worked on developing learning contracts with undergraduates and MBA students.

Laurie Thomas is Professor of Human Learning at Brunel University and Carl Rogers Memorial Professor at Clayton University. He is joint head - with Sheila Harri-Augstein - of the postgraduate division of the Centre for the Study of Human Learning. This research unit was formed in 1967 and has been using personal learning contracts as a major facet of its research since that time.

Edgar Wilson teaches philosophy and has been course leader of the Degree by Independent Study at the Crewe and Alsager Faculty, Manchester Metropolitan University since the original validation.

Glossary

APL	Assessment of Prior Learning
APEL	Assessment of Prior Experiential Learning
BTEC	Business and Technology Education Council
CATS	Credit Accumulation and Transfer Scheme
CM	Certificate in Management
CNAA	Council for National Academic Awards
DFE	Department for Education
DipHE	Diploma in Higher Education
EHE	Enterprise in Higher Education
ET	Employment Training
ERASMUS	European Community Action Scheme for the Mobility of University Students
HE	Higher Education
HEI	Higher Education Institution
HEC	Higher Education for Capability
HMI	Her Majesty's Inspectorate
HNC	Higher National Certificate
HND	Higher National Diploma
JBPVE	Joint Board for Pre-Vocational Education
LET	Learning from Experience Trust
MBA	Master of Business Administration
MSC	Manpower Services Commission
PSI	Policy Studies Institute
RSA	Royal Society for the encouragement of Arts, Manufactures and Commerce
SIS	School for Independent Study
SML	Self-Managed Learning
TEED	Training, Enterprise and Education Directorate
TQI	Total Quality Improvement
TQM	Total Quality Management
UEL	University of East London

Preface

The current interest in curriculum change sweeping through higher education - and further education - is a response to external demands for a new emphasis on the development of personal qualities and skills through students' specialist studies, ever-tightening resource constraints coupled with assessments of the quality of provision, and the accumulation of awareness of good practice in teaching and learning. Indeed, much of our awareness of how further and higher education might be improved has been with us for some time. What is new is the commitment of institutions to introduce new practices across a wide range of their courses.

A major feature of these developments is an emphasis on the development of student autonomy in learning. Rapidly changing circumstances at work and in society are putting a premium on adaptability, working together and learning from experience. In the UK, national movements such as Higher Education for Capability (an initiative of the Royal Society for the encouragement of Arts, Manufactures and Commerce [RSA] based in Leeds Metropolitan University and the University of Leeds) and the Department of Employment's Enterprise in Higher Education initiative have stimulated much innovation. In Australasia, similar pressure for enhancing the quality and relevance of provision is provoking a similar response.

Higher Education for Capability's 'Using...' series of conferences is based on the proposition that there already exists a range of ways in which these new challenges are being met. We believe that others can learn from these experiences, particularly if they are seen to be in operation and not just in somebody's imagination. Each in the series focuses on one general 'theme in practice', in this case Using Learning Contracts. We begin in Part One with a review of the general features of the theme and the reasons why many institutions are seeking to introduce it in their own programmes. In Part Two, the largest section, we present a range of examples written by people in the field based on their own experience of its use. Finally in Part Three we present a review of this experience, including the issues raised, ways forward and the potential for further development.

This series will be of interest to all with responsibility for the design and delivery of the curriculum in higher and further education. We do not present blueprints or models of good practice but present the reader with a glimpse of what others are doing and what they have learned from doing it, leaving readers to judge its relevance and adapt its implementation to their own circumstances.

The examples featured in this edition were presented at a national conference on Using Learning Contracts held at the RSA in London sponsored by the University of East London and Digital Equipment Co. Limited. Higher Education for Capability (HEC) would like to hear of other examples, particularly where they may better illustrate some of the issues.* HEC publicises examples in its National Capability and Enterprise Database which is available internationally via the Joint Academic Computer Network. The 'Using ...' series is intended to be the start of an exchange of experience which might ultimately lead to greater understanding of the processes of teaching and learning in Higher and Further Education.

* Address: Higher Education for Capability, 20 Queen Square, Leeds, LS2 8AF; telephone 0532 347725, facsimile 0532 442025.

Part One:

The Context

Chapter One

Learning Contracts: Scope and Rationale

John Stephenson and Mike Laycock

Introduction

Interest in the use of learning contracts in further and higher education is rising rapidly. In response to an invitation from Higher Education for Capability (HEC), University of East London (UEL) and Digital Equipment Company Ltd, 200 people assembled in London in February 1992 to explore the theoretical and practical aspects of using learning contracts in higher education. Thirty examples of current practice were presented. This book draws on the evidence presented at that conference and formulates some propositions about the nature and possible future uses of learning contracts across a wide spectrum of situations.

What are learning contracts?

For the uninitiated the term 'learning contract' might imply a legalistic, bureaucratic approach to learning. A 'negotiated learning plan' might better express both the processes and methods involved. Learning contracts are agreements negotiated between students and staff and, where appropriate, employers, regarding the type and amount of study to be undertaken and the type and amount of assessment or credit resulting from this study. They are not contracts in the legal sense but indicate a commitment of the parties to the study or learning involved. They can cover any period of time and can be used with varying degrees of formality or academic legitimacy for a variety of institutional and/or off-campus learning and with individuals or groups of students. Typically, they involve students in negotiating their learning goals, the methods by which those goals will be met and the means by which the achievement of the goals can be assessed and at what level.

The Educational Function of Learning Contracts

Learning contracts appear to have two major functions. First, they provide a mechanism for managing the great variety of learning activities negotiated between students and others. Second, the process of planning, negotiating and completing learning contracts is a valuable learning experience in its own right. This book is primarily concerned with the second of these functions.

There are at least five ways in which the use of learning contracts has educational pay-offs for students:

a) they help students recognise and clarify the roles of the different stakeholders in their educational development, such as tutors, employers and fellow-students;
b) they provide opportunities for students to develop a strong sense of ownership of their studies;
c) they raise the quality of students' learning experiences by helping them to clarify their learning goals, to reflect on their learning and to address issues of assessment of performance;
d) they provide excellent opportunities for effective collaboration – between students and students, students and teachers, students and employers - on matters directly relevant to each student's education;
e) they help students develop a range of useful skills and build confidence in their own ability and personal effectiveness.

More specifically, learning contracts require *students* to:

a) be explicit about their learning intentions;
b) set clear and achievable goals;
c) justify their plans in terms of their own personal, vocational and/or academic development;
d) develop their communication, decision-making and evaluative skills;
e) address key issues such as the level of performance required to secure external accreditation.

There is much evidence from student, teacher and employer testimony that involving students in the design of their own programmes of study improves the quality of their learning, increases motivation, promotes understanding of fundamentals and focuses student attention on the wider relevance of their studies. The greater the scale of responsibility - for complete modules or even for complete programmes - the greater the potential academic and personal benefits for the students.

The benefits of using learning contracts extend to other parties to a contract. For courses with a strong vocational orientation, learning contracts enable *employers* to:

a) participate in the development of student plans;
b) plan more effective work placements;
c) target student sponsorship more precisely;
d) spot and recruit talent early;
e) reassure students on the relevance of their programmes.

A learning contract approach requires *course teams* to:

a) be explicit about their own assumptions, about what they are prepared to negotiate, and the criteria they will use for approving contracts;
b) establish criteria and procedures for securing approvals from external bodies and which enable students to renegotiate their programmes in response to progress and any unanticipated learning;
c) provide an environment of intellectual rigour and continuing personal support within which students can prepare their plans, review their progress and complete their programmes.

Learning contracts are a way of providing public credibility for programmes of study negotiated by students. Legitimate interests can be given a stake in the student's programme. Students can set out their proposals; employers and/or accrediting bodies can signify (or decline to signify) their approval. Once approval has been secured, students and their tutors can proceed with the programme confident that its successful completion will be fully recognised.

The current debate on learning contracts in higher education

The parties concerned with the 1992 Using Learning Contracts conference, Higher Education for Capability, University of East London, and Digital Equipment Co. Limited, have themselves played a significant part in the promotion of the idea and practice of learning contracts.

Contribution of Higher Education for Capability (HEC)

Since 1980, the Royal Society for the encouragement of Arts, Manufactures and Commerce (RSA) has called for radical changes in the way education prepares people for life after school and university. The RSA's Education for Capability Manifesto, issued in 1980, asserted that:

> a well-balanced education should, of course, embrace the analysis and acquisition of knowledge. But it must also include the exercise of creative skills, the competence to undertake and complete tasks and the ability to cope with everyday life; and also doing all these things in co-operation with others. (RSA, 1980)

Established in 1988, Higher Education for Capability (HEC) has taken the debate identified in the 'Education for Capability Manifesto' into higher education to challenge the scepticism which the Manifesto initially raised in some sections and to support good practice. Since then HEC, through debates with over 70 higher education institutions, has helped establish a consensus that an effective way of combining the development of student capability with the pursuit of academic excellence is to give students experience of being responsible and accountable for their own educational development.

HEC argued that because graduates would need to be able to flourish within ever-changing circumstances, at work, in the community and in their personal lives, they should develop the capacity to participate in change, to cope with change, to manage their own changing circumstances and to take responsibility for their own progress through those circumstances as part of their undergraduate education. If students were to be adequately prepared to be responsible and accountable for their own continuing development after graduation, the HEC argument continued, they ought to have experience of being responsible and accountable for their own development before graduation.

At the time, many in HE saw the demand to develop student capability as making extra demands on their valuable time; that time given to the development of the skills and qualities of 'doing' would detract from their real business of helping students with 'the knowing'. Now, an increasing number of people in higher education understand that the twin demands of knowing and doing are complementary not competitive, and that both can be achieved within the context of students' mainstream studies. HEC has argued that it is a matter of the nature of the student's learning experiences, that if students are required to be passive receivers of teacher-delivered material, they will remain passive participants in a world of change and that if they are required to take initiatives and to be responsible and accountable for what they learn, they will be better prepared to manage change and their continuing development after they leave.

The HEC campaign for students to be given more responsibility for their own learning raised a number of concerns amongst many academics: 'students may learn the wrong things, may set their sights too low or too high, may make too many demands of meagre resources, may miss out on employment opportunities, may dodge the difficult bits, may not know how to proceed, may choose the easy way, will be irresponsible'. These concerns were also raised by some students, particularly if they had had no previous experience of responsibility.

HEC advocates the use of learning contracts as a way of addressing these understandable concerns. Learning contracts require students to be accountable as well as responsible for their own learning, and give other relevant stakeholders, such as teachers, HE institutions, employers and the community, direct involvement in student decision-making. Moreover learning contracts, if signed by institutions, employers and accrediting bodies reassure students that work which they themselves have planned will be recognised by others.

Learning contracts, in other words, give a structure within which students can learn how to be responsible for their own development; they put the emphasis on reflection on action, not on action alone. They also help students develop personal transferable skills within the context of their mainstream studies. Teachers and employers have to rethink their roles; they too have to be accountable for their contributions and be explicit about the judgements they make.

Contribution of Enterprise in Higher Education

A parallel and overlapping initiative which has also had a significant role in the growing debate about the use of learning contracts has been the Enterprise in Higher Education (EHE) initiative launched by the Secretary of State for Employment in 1987 with the support of the Secretaries of State for Education and Science, Trade and Industry, Scotland and Wales. EHE aims to assist institutions of higher education develop enterprising graduates in partnership with employers. Higher education institutions throughout England, Scotland and Wales were invited to bid for funding of specific enterprise plans of up to £1 million spread over five years. Over 60 institutions are now involved in the initiative.

Like Higher Education for Capability, EHE has placed considerable emphasis on the value of giving students responsibility for their own learning. EHE seeks to effect curriculum change which is predominantly process- rather than content-related and which is oriented towards two specific themes: the move towards active, experiential learning styles and the relevance of the curriculum to the world of work.

Throughout its literature EHE refers to the importance of increasing 'student responsibility in learning'. The Employment Department document publicising the 'Key Features of Enterprise in Higher Education' (1991) clarifies the philosophy, stating that:

> Traditional teaching methods are giving way to more participative and activity-based styles, where enterprising qualities are encouraged and rewarded. Students need increasingly to develop responsibility for their own lifelong learning. (p. 1)

The accent on this shift towards student responsibility in learning is also identified in a recent National Foundation for Educational Research (1991) survey of institutions involved in the enterprise initiative:

> The shift in focus implies a shift in teaching and learning strategies away from the traditional transmissive mode of formal lectures towards an emphasis on students' responsibility for their own learning...(where)...students would construct knowledge rather than receive it; would do so with greater independence and opportunity to work in small groups and would be assessed by procedures which acknowledge the nature and context of their learning. (p. 93)

For many, the educational philosophy and practice explicit in this shift from a pedagogical to an andrological model is very familiar and something to which Malcolm Knowles (1986), in his work on learning contracts, has consistently referred.

The contribution of Digital Equipment Co Limited (UK)

Digital Equipment Co Limited (DEC) is one of many major companies concerned about the ability of new graduates to cope with the pressures and complexity of working in a rapidly changing environment. Students, they argue, do not seem to have the necessary personal qualities and skills which will enable them to cope with the management of change. Accordingly, DEC has encouraged and helped many institutions of higher education to introduce more participative approaches on their courses and has joined a number of EHE Steering Committees, including UEL's, Enterprise Committee. DEC's enthusiasm for learning contracts is shown by their support for the Using Learning Contracts conference and for the preparation of this book.

Widening participation

The late 1980s and early 1990s have seen an acceleration in the rate of growth in student numbers. This acceleration has been motivated as much by resource concerns as by a desire to widen access. Whatever its cause, the expansion of student numbers has been accompanied by the shift towards giving students more responsibility for their own learning, as described above. Many have come to realise that the drive towards massive expansion in student numbers without, necessarily, a commensurate increase in staffing or capital expenditure must inevitably lead to a changed conceptual framework of teaching and learning. The emerging framework is dependent on reducing traditional contact time and increasing the development of self-managed or self-directed learning. Coupled with this is the move towards more open or resource-based learning taking advantage of new technologies such as CD ROM, interactive video and specific software applications such as 'Hypertext'. Institutions are increasingly viewing themselves less as directors of the educational experience and more as resources enabling learning to take place. Some of the expansion of student numbers is being achieved through post-experience programmes for work-based part-time students for whom a more work-related and flexible provision is required. Among the many reforms suggested by Sir Christopher Ball in his report, *More means Different* (1990), is that:

> Active, participative learning must replace passive education. Students need help to become responsible for their own learning...New modes of delivery make possible a new relationship between the teacher and student. (p. 43)

New relationships, a new culture

The use of learning contracts invites new relationships between students, teachers and employers and implies a new culture in higher education. Whilst new relationships are clearly possible - as illustrated by the many examples available - successfully achieving them in practice is often the most difficult aspect of change. Academic staff have traditionally controlled all aspects of learning including what is to be learnt, how it is to be learnt, when and where it is to be learnt and how it is to be assessed. In more conventional approaches, it is staff who take responsibility for the learning rather than the learner. The learning contract places the student in the role of initiator and learning manager, and the staff in counselling, supportive, responsive, expert, resource gate-keeping and feedback-giving roles.

The use of learning contracts has the potential for promoting a more participative, democratic partnership between student and institution, a partnership that can be negotiated and which includes a notion of quality by contract rather than quality by control. Learning contracts do more than facilitate student responsibility and accountability in learning. Their use challenges traditional views of education and requires staff, students and employers to re-think their roles and responsibilities and to question the purpose of higher education.

One EHE learning contracts example

One institution, The University of East London, has responded to the EHE call for more student responsibility and effective partnerships with employers by making learning contracts the main feature of its EHE programme. The aims of the University's Enterprise Learning Programme are:

a) to facilitate in all courses throughout the University, the development of a learning process which actively encourages students as individuals and as members of learning groups, to take greater responsibility for their own learning, and
b) to create a learning environment in which the approval and assessment of students' programmes of study are conducted in partnership between the student, the institution and employers/practitioners.

The use of learning contracts therefore features strongly in the University's EHE Programme. Many Faculty projects have been funded which identify their use, for example in project work, placement and work experience. The learning contract has become an important mechanism in realising the aims of the Programme.

There are three reasons why learning contracts appealed to the UEL Enterprise programme. First, they raise the quality of the students' learning experiences by challenging them to set learning objectives, to define the criteria by which that learning is to be judged and to engage in a learning cycle of planning, monitoring and reviewing learning. That cycle not only has strong theoretical support, it is also good professional practice.

Second, depending on how the learning contract is structured, there is the possibility of subsuming within it many of the current educational developments such as the Assessment of Prior Experiential Learning, Portfolios, Profiling and Records of Achievement. One such structure has five simple questions which can be asked with increasing degrees of sophistication up to postgraduate level:

First, where have I been?
This invites a critical review of the student's life, work and educational experience.
Second, where am I now?
This involves the student in appraising strengths and weaknesses in knowledge, skills and experience.
Third, where do I want to get to?
This requires the student to set out longer-term aims and objectives for the programme of study.
Fourth, how am I going to get there?
This question requires the student to describe the specific content,

the wider context, the skills development required, a timetable and the resources required presented in the form of an action plan.
Fifth, how will I know that I have arrived?
This invites the student to propose the means by which the achievement of the course objectives will be demonstrated.

The third reason why the University has embraced learning contracts is that they provide the means by which the student, the institution and employers can negotiate, approve and assess the outcomes of study whilst both institution and employer act as a resource for learning. Figure 1.1 illustrates this tripartite process of negotiation, approval and assessment.

Figure 1.1 shows how the student has a central role in a) negotiating the learning contract with the institution and the employer, b) implementing the

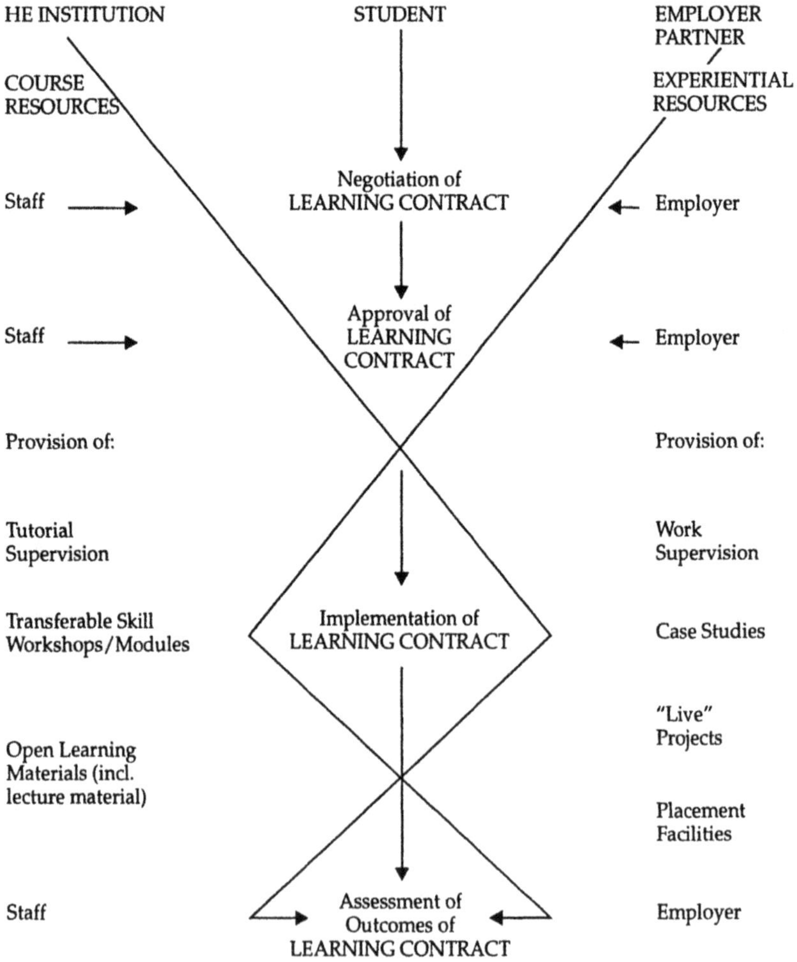

Figure 1.1 *Partnership in the learning contract*

learning contract and c) the tripartite assessment of the outcomes. The institution provides a range of resources including tutorial supervision, workshops and open learning or resource-based materials, including lecture materials. A wide range of experiential resources can be provided by the employer such as work supervision, mentoring, case studies, live projects and placement facilities.

The University of East London's agreement with the Employment Department indicates that over 7000 students will use learning contracts for a specifiable part of their course by the end of the five-year period. It is an ambitious programme. The University sees learning contracts not only as a means of introducing a more participative democracy into higher education but also as a means by which students can become possessors of sound knowledge, confident in their own ability, confident at working with others and capable of initiating and implementing effective action.

References

Ball, Sir Christopher (1990) *More Means Different*, London: RSA.

Employment Department Group (1990-91) *Enterprise in Higher Education: Key Features of Enterprise in Higher Education*, Sheffield: EDG.

Knowles, M S (1986) *Using Learning Contracts*, San Francisco, CA: Jossey-Bass.

National Foundation for Educational Research (NFER) (1991) *Enterprise in Higher Education, Final Report*, March, Windsor: NFER.

Royal Society for the encouragement of Arts, Manufactures and Commerce (RSA) (1990) *Education for Capability Manifesto*, London: RSA.

Part Two:

The Experience

SECTION ONE: LEARNING CONTRACTS AND NEGOTIATION

Introduction

Mike Laycock and John Stephenson

Learning contracts, unlike legal contracts, imply involvement in a negotiative process. For the majority of students entering higher education and, indeed, those involved in learning at any stage of their lives, the expectation surrounding the process of teaching and learning is, from important historical antecedents, governed by the practice of pedagogy. A pedagogical model implies that the teacher takes a primary role in ownership and control of the educative process and, thereby, responsibility for it. The androgogical model, by contrast implies a more cooperative, dialectical learning process encouraging experiential and autonomous learning and the empowerment of the learner. The growth of current techniques in higher education which explicitly require students to engage in processes which enable them to plan, monitor and review learning progress and accepting more autonomy, as Knowles (1981) has observed, is unfamiliar territory for many staff:

> There is an urgent need for all programmes of higher education... to be geared (from the start) to developing the skills of autonomous learning... (with subsequent units being) designed as self-directed learning activities. This is to say that the new emphasis in higher education must be on the *process of learning*, with the *acquisition of content* (rather than the transmission of content) being a natural (but not pre-programmed) result.
>
> To re-orientate higher education...in this direction would be a tremendous challenge. It is a concept foreign to most educators. It has not been part of their training.... It requires a redefinition of their role away from that of transmitter and controller of instruction to that of facilitator and resource person to self-directed learners. It is frightening. They do not know how to do it. (p. 8)

The practices promoted by EHE and Higher Education for Capability initiatives have focused attention not only on the relationship between students and staff but on a wider political level of the relationship between individual and institutional expectations. Hammond and Collins (1991), for example, have already given this agenda priority:

> Educators committed to justice and personal freedom from oppression...(should) build a co-operative learning climate, rather than perpetuating or tolerating a conventional learning climate, with its stated and unstated assumptions of teachers and the teaching institution being in complete control .... As we see it, the ultimate purpose of building a co-operative learning climate is to provide a basis for experimentation with and critical reflection on, alternative power relations. (pp. 23-4)

It is this kind of critical reflection on a cooperative, negotiative learning process, engendered through the use of a learning contract, that has informed the work of contributors to this section.

Mac McCarthy identifies four factors affecting negotiation; the organisational view of education, the established view of organisational operation, the personal challenges to teachers and the limits to negotiation exacted by course demands. The highlighting of the organisational perspective serves to illustrate that negotiating the educative process is not solely dependent on the ability of staff or student to manage an alternative relationship. The prevailing institutional ethos may either support, deny or at least be antipathetic to such a cultural shift in learning styles. Considering all forms of potential constraint, McCarthy then identifies those aspects of the learning environment upon which there might be a 'range of negotiability'.

From practice at the University of Central England in Birmingham Institute of Art and Design, Tom Jones similarly identifies the place of the learning contract in formulating a study programme which brings together 'institutional and individual perspectives, simultaneously respecting the individual's context and intentions and institutional standards and expectations'. Crucially, Jones also refers to the importance in the negotiation process of enabling students to respect their 'previous achievements and current learning aims' where there might be a 'cultural mis-match' between the objectives and requirements of student and institution, often unrecognised as potentially damaging.

Piper and Wilson set institutional expectations within a broader framework. Their contribution emphasises the importance of 'shared and explicit understandings and procedures' which clearly meet institutional requirements so that students have a 'reasonable awareness of both relevant procedures and regulations and also of the academic and conceptual framework within which they are intending to work'. Students undertaking Independent Project Planning prepare a highly structured learning contract or Proposal which is submitted to a Registration Board for consideration. The composition of the Board ensures not only external peer judgement 'but also confers "respectability" to what could otherwise be considered a dangerously untraditional activity'. Approval of the Proposal is dependent on satisfying criteria which 'are both rigorous and extensive'. Students are required to submit formal progress review reports to a Course Qualification Committee and their work is assessed against agreements made at registration. Highly formalised institutional mechanisms have been established which not only recognise and mirror the cycle of planning, monitoring and reviewing undertaken by the student but satisfy and secure institutional demands for accountability in the changed power relationship.

Though very similar processes and institutional procedures have characterised the operation of Independent Study at the University of East London, Dave O'Reilly concentrates more specifically on the wider implications of institutional organization and its consequences for the negotiation of individual programmes of study during the history of the most experienced provision of independent learning. Though originally conceived as integral to institutional development, Independent Study became perceived as separate from the University with issues of shared ownership and marginalisation closely linked to resources. Tensions within the School for Independent Study resulting from competing educational definitions are also seen as creating instability. The critical HMI report in 1990 has led to a radical re-organisation of its operation resulting in a return to the original organisational vision with devolution supported by a small Coordinating Unit. Despite this institutional turbulence, O'Reilly concludes that 'learning contracts (may have) scarcely scratched the surface of their potential in education.'

References

Knowles, M S (1981) 'Preface'. In Boud, D. (ed.) *Developing Student Autonomy in Learning*, London: Kogan Page.

Hammond, M and Collins, R (1991) *Self-Directed Learning: Critical Practice*, London: Kogan Page.

Chapter Two

Factors Affecting Negotiation

Mac McCarthy

Traditionally, teachers have had control of what goes on in the classroom and students have surrendered their freedom of choice after making the initial decision to do the course. There is a long history of education to give legitimacy to this situation; teachers have been (and, indeed, still are) seen by themselves and their students as experts. In addition, since the earliest days of formal education, discipline and control have been an essential principle of the hidden curriculum. These developments have ensured a relationship between teacher and learner which is unequal and, therefore, potentially limiting for the learner.

The essential irony today is that the power of the expert is being eroded by a number of sources, not least of which is the Government, but the demand for discipline and control is no less strong. Alongside calls for adaptable and flexible learners who can handle change in their working lives and adapt through learning, education is still seen to play a role in the process of social control. Typically, teachers react by reasserting their authority in the classroom. An additional dimension to that irony is that, particularly in higher education, students largely remain in awe of the expertise with which they are confronted, regardless of its erosion elsewhere. They still attribute their inability to understand a lecture to the genius of the teacher and the latter's consequent inability to 'speak our language'.

My concern is for the learner in such a confused milieu, especially since the demands upon him or her are changing radically, but I believe that, in making proposals to redress the balance of power in the learning relationship, the teacher will also benefit.

Negotiation in the classroom is hardly a new idea, although one might think so from the poor headway that has been made to date. Negotiation allows the learner to make decisions, in consultation with and by agreement with, the teacher. It is thus a process of empowerment and a way of developing learner responsibility. The role of the teacher becomes more facilitative. However, initially, the onus is upon the teacher to set up the negotiation process and to give it legitimacy.

Factors affecting negotiability

The ability of the teacher to negotiate is affected by:

a) the established view of education within the organisation;
b) the established view of how the organisation operates;
c) personal factors which influence the extent to which the teacher feels comfortable negotiating with learners;
d) the demands of the course which define the limits of what can be negotiated and to what extent.

I want to examine each of these in turn for their influence on the negotiation process.

Perspectives on education

A useful comparison of the changing perspectives on education was provided by Margaret Levi in 1983, as part of some research undertaken on behalf of the Manpower Services Commission (MSC). She examined the structures of existing curricula, together with the requirements for the future; her model of the traditional curriculum revealed the following assumptions:

a) known content and skills;
b) knowledge and personal development are separated;
c) occupational change is deemed to be unlikely;
d) skills taught relate to a known 'product'.

She contrasted this with a new perspective based upon recognition that curricular issues have to respond to a changing world. This view was based upon radically different assumptions:

a) anticipated changes of employer;
b) education and training for flexibility, adaptability and transferability;
c) the accepted importance of process learning;
d) holistic approaches to learning and teaching.

In practice, it is not a clear-cut choice between one model and the other; rather, there is a continuum and even within one college views will differ between individuals and between groups. It is important to recognise, however, that the groups who are debating these issues include college managers, team leaders, teachers and learners. Beyond the confines of college, employers are also part of the debate. Educationally, important contributions have been made to the discussion by educational bodies, such as the Business and Technician Education Council (BTEC), the Joint Board for Pre-Vocational Education (JBPVE) and the Department for Education (DFE). Many of the policy documents that emerged in the 1980s reflected the 'new' view described by Margaret Levi. The MSC, too, advocated this view, although, as the Training, Enterprise and Education Directorate (TEED), it may well be that, in practice, it gives the lie to this espoused view as the effects of many of the more dubious training organisations become known. Many of the organisations which have sprung up in response to the Employment Training (ET) programme adopt a very narrow view of training which is educationally questionable and reductionist.

The prevailing view within a particular institution, or even a part of that institution, will affect the ability of the teacher to implement any system of negotiation. It will be necessary for that teacher, therefore, to be aware of any mismatch between personal and organisational views, to define those areas where adjustment may be needed, and to decide where negotiation can fruitfully take place between teacher and learner. It may well be that these issues have to be negotiated first between the teacher and a member of the management team.

Perspectives on the organization

For the purposes of developing a programme of negotiated learning, four views are relevant here:

a) how management thinks the organisation operates;
b) how the teacher, working in it, perceives it;
c) how the learner, learning in it, perceives it;
d) how it actually works.

Factors which affect the ability to negotiate include: the degree of autocracy within the organisation, the pervasiveness and strength of bureaucracy, the amount of democracy and involvement (both in planning and implementing courses), the effectiveness of communication, and the prevailing culture both within and without the organisation.

It is important for the teacher to identify the extent to which he or she works for the organisation or is part of it. He or she needs to know how much room there is for negotiation and on what topics; what are acceptable and unacceptable areas for negotiation need identifying. It is equally important for future development to establish the reasons why certain areas are deemed unacceptable.

Personal factors in negotiation

The teacher faces a number of personal challenges in tackling the problem of classroom negotiated learning. Not least are those to do with what is personally comfortable in a classroom relationship. Most teachers have fears about some aspect of teaching, some of which are irrational but some of which are well-founded. One's view of oneself inside and outside the classroom is important. Similarly, the view one has of the learner as a person is vital for setting the parameters of negotiation, for negotiation is a process between human beings and therefore subject to the dangers and pitfalls of any other kind of interpersonal interaction. Various views have prevailed in the past and, indeed, still find favour in many colleges. All too often the student is still perceived as an essentially passive receptacle for knowledge handed down by the teacher as expert. Alternatively, the student is an extension of a mechanistic process called learning, so that although active, the student resembles a robot, regurgitating knowledge when required to do so. Occasionally, the learner is a 'slave' to the supremacy of the teacher. Less frequently than one might imagine, the learner is an adult actively engaged in a mutually rewarding and active relationship.

It is, therefore, important that teachers develop a high degree of self-awareness. Important questions to ask include:

What am I comfortable with, in terms of classroom interaction?
What am I uncomfortable with?
What fears do I have about teaching?
How many of these are founded on fact?
How do I perceive myself in the classroom?
How do I think the students perceive me?
How do I perceive the students?

Even more importantly, college managers need to recognise that there is an important staff development task here. Staff need to have the opportunity to explore such issues through appropriate self-development mechanisms.

Course demands

Every course involves an uneasy mix of curricular demands, administrative procedures and resource constraints. Within these broad parameters, there are assessment issues, teaching methodology and course philosophy to consider. The resulting mix creates a complex situation which can severely limit the ability of tutors to introduce genuine negotiation into the learning experience. Even so, in every course there are boundaries where the issues are less clearly unfolded and exploration of these boundaries may reveal opportunities to consider, at least, some means of negotiation.

Every course, particularly those associated with the so-called new initiatives mentioned earlier, divides its demands upon tutors and learners into content and process. Achieving a balance between them involves a degree of negotiation, though this is often worked out in the mind of the tutor. Adopting a recursive approach, one can see that negotiation may, itself, provide a useful vehicle for encouraging both content and process learning.

Areas of negotiation

At some point the all-important question has to be addressed: what, precisely, can be negotiated in the classroom, given the constraints established by consideration of the issues outlined above? It is important to remember that the issue is never a straight choice between 'negotiable' and 'non-negotiable'. In all cases there has to be a range of negotiability, constrained in part by the organisation, the prevailing view of education and the personal capabilities of both the teacher and the learner. It is, nevertheless, possible to establish some degree of negotiation on:

a) course content;
b) course process;
c) learning and teaching methodology;
d) method of assessment;
e) assessment process;
f) course evaluation;
g) control and discipline.

This gets well away from the traditional view of the learner's role where his or her control is largely abandoned after making the initial choice of course of study.

Negotiation skills

If the notion of classroom negotiation is to become acceptable and viable, one of the major prerequisites must be staff development because there will be a degree of resistance and, at the very least, some uncertainty. Negotiation requires the development of a number of competences, some of which are listed in brief below:

a) establishing the bargaining area;
b) establishing the negotiating range;
c) valuing the other person(s) involved;
d) identifying the objectives;
e) listening more than you talk;
f) being neutral and factual;
g) actively seeking mutual acceptability;
h) knowing the concessions that you can make;
i) identifying and using a colleague to discuss the issues with (a co-counsellor or mentor).

Finally, it is worth considering the benefits and difficulties that there are for both staff and students – this may well be the starting point!

Acknowledgements

I am indebted to J Kidd of Management Training Systems for his understanding of negotiation skills, which he was generous enough to share with me.

An earlier version of this article was published in the *Journal for Further and Higher Education*, **15**, 1, Spring 1991.

Chapter Three

Negotiation as a Learning Tool for Tutors and Students

Tom Jones

The Birmingham Institute of Art and Design at the University of Central England has developed the use of informal contracts in access studies for adult students over a period of five years, and for similar students at undergraduate (Diploma in Higher Education [DipHE]) level for three years. However, the term 'contract' has been carefully avoided, since its legalistic overtones would be alien to the spirit of negotiation, the learning method employed for both levels of study. The Institute's experience in this field is more than subject-specific and has general implications for the design of student-centred learning for adults.

Study programmes

Each student is required to write a programme of study that needs to be formally approved as an individual course. These programmes are far more than shopping lists of student requirements in that they constitute past, present and future surveys of the students' own capabilities, intentions and needs. Written during the early phases of study, they constitute the outcome of an initial study skills unit comprising orientation, lengthy discussions and counselling, study opportunity sampling and self-analysis. The validation of the study programme by course tutors, with external moderation, forms the assessment of the study skills unit. Learning achievement is assessed at the conclusion of each subsequent unit according to pre-established criteria, and on the evidence of unit products.

Functions

Programme writing for students is a process of self-discovery, a confidence-building exercise, a means of identifying their learning aims, and a statement of how they wish to use what the Institute can offer.

Programme writing for tutors is a means of understanding each student's background, perspectives, needs and potential. It also enables them to guide students toward the level of expected achievement and to ensure that the quality of learning is being maintained. In practical terms, resource needs can be specified and planned, a process which is especially important in the current climate and in cases where students are planning to include a high proportion of independent study or fieldwork.

The overarching function of the study programme is to bring together institutional and individual perspectives, simultaneously respecting the individual's context and intentions, and institutional standards and capabilities.

Issues

The main theme linking most of the issues that have arisen in the operation of negotiated study through programme writing is the concept of shared learning. Programmes present neither a list of demands to the institution, nor impose a list of requirements on the students. Programme writing has enabled this confrontational approach in learning to be, if not eliminated, at least contained and neutralised.

Study programmes must be flexible enough to respond to evolution and change in students' learning capacities and opportunities. They must also be specific enough to form a framework for identifiable individual development and progression of learning, consistent with institutional expectations. The critical and academic discipline entailed in achieving and articulating this balance both establishes and strengthens students' sense of owning their studies.

More specifically for tutors, guiding students through programme writing helps them develop more respect for their previous achievements and current learning aims. This is particularly important where issues of cultural mis-match between institution and student are concerned. Experience with negotiated study has shown these to be much more widespread, and more damaging to students, than tutors usually understand. Again this contributes to the quality of shared learning, and is in effect a form of staff development.

Summary

While a neat summing up of what has been learnt through operating study programmes would be neither easy nor useful, three central elements can be picked out:

a) the operation of negotiated programmes of study needs to relate to each institution's established circumstances, ethos and practice;

b) if such agreements are to be productive in developing capability in higher education, they should be based on a tutor/student partnership that students can recognise; otherwise, they could become another form of an authoritarian approach to teaching and learning;

c) while something of the same format can be used, study agreements need to be clearly distinguished from course documents as traditionally written since they are collaborative, owned by the student and flexible enough to guide and respond to his or her development in learning. This implies that study programmes, far from being prescriptive in planning and restrictive in curriculum control, become a means of development beyond expectations and a vehicle for bringing new study concepts into higher education.

Chapter Four

Negotiating Complete Programmes of Study

John Piper and Edgar Wilson

Learning contracts and independent study

Context

The BA (Hons) Applied Social Studies (by Independent Study) at Crewe and Alsager Faculty, Manchester Metropolitan University was approved by the Council for National Academic Awards (CNAA) in 1981. Determined effort by the course team convinced largely traditionalist validators of the legitimacy of undergraduate honours-level independent study, conducted in an 'ex-teacher training college'. This persistence and subsequent successful implementation received an early recognition when the Royal Society of Arts bestowed its Education for Capability Award on the course in 1982. After ten years of successful operation, the course received a glowing report following a substantial inspection by Her Majesty's Inspectorate (HMI) during the Autumn term 1991.

The course was designed to operate within a pre-existent modular degree scheme including around 30 subject patterns at the Diploma in Higher Education (DipHE) stage and a number of linked honours awards. Students following the course are able to select from a number of units and patterns in years one and two to achieve the DipHE, but the honours award is based entirely on work in year three. This consists almost exclusively of an independent study project.

The course is offered in both full-time and part-time modes and has persistently attracted a student group of which over 60 per cent are mature, over 50 per cent are female, and over 50 per cent enter college without standard entry qualifications. There is clear evidence that independent study, in combination with an explicit learning contract, provides these students with a course appropriate for real personal and academic development. It has also consistently delivered positive vocational outcomes.

Rationale and structure

The commitment of The Royal Society of Arts to Education for Capability is mirrored by the explicit philosophy of the course. Just as the concept of capability denies the distinction between theory and practice, so the course encourages students to focus on the application and testing of knowledge in practical settings. From a particular reading of Popper (1965), the course team derived a central commitment to the idea that while students engaged in independent study should be encouraged to question received wisdom and to follow their personal interests, this can only be achieved from a foundation of established disciplinary knowledge and academic confidence. This approach is not encouraging to potential students who would wish to follow purely idiosyncratic paths to personal fulfilment or to re-invent familiar objects or systems of thought. Following Durkheim, it is axiomatic that relationships of contract are dependent on the existence of shared knowledge, values and assumptions. In relation to learning contracts this means that students cannot enter into a meaningful contract without a reasonable awareness of both relevant procedures and regulations and also of the academic and conceptual framework within which they are intending to work. To permit them to do so would appear to be both unwise and unprofessional.

From these principles the course is structured so as to offer students in years one and two a choice of patterns including Sociology and Psychology (as core disciplines), Youth and Community Studies, Health Studies, Special Needs, Philosophy, and Business Education. Alongside these subject patterns the student must follow a number of compulsory units concerned with inquiry skills, the development of competence in self-directed inquiry and the development and completion of independent projects. These are essential units designed to ensure that the student will be ready to work successfully at an appropriate level during the third year with its bias towards independent study. Additionally, a number of units are available which focus on relevant transferable skills, such as 'Reason and Argument', and 'Communication and Group Behaviour'. A balance is thus sought between the development of a secure foundation in disciplinary and applied academic studies and in the general and particular skills required for successful independent work.

Independent project planning (contract development)

The compulsory 'Independent Project Module' in year two involves the student in the development of a detailed project proposal for their work in year three. Students are encouraged to contact any member of the course team to discuss drafts of this proposal. A record of this negotiation and consultation is kept which includes summaries of the main points covered at each stage. Students are also encouraged to consider the involvement of external agencies both for placement purposes and also for possible supervision and assessment. The area of negotiation includes assessment, since it is recognised that this can be varied both in mode and weighting to fit the nature of the particular independent project. The criteria for the approval of independent projects, which run to four pages, are available to both staff and students. They are derived from well-established CNAA principles relating to honours work at undergraduate level and require that a project should necessitate the demonstration of intellectual development, understanding and competence, critical judgement, communication skills, and synthesis across a broad cognitive perspective.

Out of these shared and explicit understandings and procedures, the student is required to produce an Independent Project Proposal which is the basis of the learning contract. This proposal document, which is supported by further detail in relation to both academic and practical implications of the project, requires that students specify the nature of the topic, its rationale, their relevant prior experience and academic record, their aims and objectives for the project and its implications for subsequent career intentions, the nature of the competences and skills which will be developed, the external contacts required and agreed, the relevant resources required, the structure, content, and methods involved in the actual project, the nature of assessment both in terms of its mode and weighting and the total workload in relation to a conventional course. This requirement is not easily met and will typically be a focus of student attention over five or six months preceding the submission of the Independent Project Proposal to the Registration Board for consideration.

Project registration (contract agreement)

The Registration Board is distinct from the Course Examination Board and is convened solely for the purpose of vetting and approving Independent Project Proposals. It includes all members of the course team, other appropriate college tutors and also a number of external members. The inclusion of distinguished external academics and senior professionals ensures external peer judgement and also confers 'respectability' to what could otherwise be considered to be a dangerously untraditional activity. It is much harder for a traditionalistic charge to be made that the course offers a context in which 'anything goes' when it can be demonstrated that 'nothing goes' unless it is agreed by a Registration Board including senior members from both academia and relevant professional areas.

Following the consideration of submissions, the Registration Board is able to approve, approve with conditions or to reject each proposal. In every case a detailed written report of the views of the Registration Board (covering both academic and practical issues) is given to the student. The criteria applied by the Registration Board are both rigorous and extensive. Thus questions are asked as to whether the project is intrinsically worthwhile and also whether the particular student will be able to complete it in the available time and within available resources. The decisions of the Registration Board are reached on the basis of the consideration of the lengthy Independent Project Proposal and also the outcome of a discussion with the student by a Board member (who is not a member of the course team) during which the student will be given the opportunity to respond to problems and issues raised in relation to their proposal. The Registration Board typically meets during July and again in more truncated form during September to consider re-submitted proposals.

Project supervision (contract support)

In relation to each Independent Project Proposal, the Registration Board is required to consider whether the College (with or without external assistance) is able to provide appropriate supervision, and the nature of that supervision is specified. There are clear guidelines available to staff and students in relation to supervision, intended to ensure a high degree of consistency and comparability of student experience. It is important that a student engaged in independent study should not be considered to be 'more expensive' than others following more traditional courses and the issue of contact time between students and supervisors receives detailed attention.

Most projects involve work-place experience and fieldwork external to the college. While there is no college commitment to providing 'supervised fieldwork' for the purposes of the course, the relevant feedback from the employer or responsible professional is always sought. Where students have been approved to follow independent projects which are beyond the supervisory resources of the course team, there have been many examples of successful external input. Thus the role of contributors from outside higher education includes not only project registration but project supervision and subsequently assessment. This provides increased responsiveness to student interests, and also affirms that there are valuable sources of personal and professional education outside higher education institutions. In this context senior social workers, principals of residential establishments, community psychiatric nurses, and even a BBC radio journalist/producer have been employed to offer specific supervision in appropriate cases. Carefully briefed, they have been able to make a valuable contribution to both supervision and assessment.

Student progress with independent project work is systematically monitored by supervisors. All students are required formally to submit to the Course Qualification Committee an interim progress review report, endorsed by their supervisor, mid-way through the final year. During the year, students are able to make changes to their registered schemes, subject to the approval of their supervisor and the Committee.

Project assessment (contract appraisal)

At the end of year three the project is assessed as specified in the contract. The mode, content and weighting of assessed work will have been agreed at the time of registration (or as modified through formal procedures) and any failure to submit work for assessment as agreed will have a negative effect. Thus, work of considerable quality may be relatively undervalued if it falls outside the agreed contract. In order to maintain comparability of standards and homogeneity of value across a wide range of projects, assessment is conducted on the basis of well-defined guidelines using general criteria related to level of performance, again derived from CNAA principles. Given the variation between projects (in relation to subject, mode and weighting of assessment) and also the large number of college tutors and external contributors, the application of such detailed criteria is essential.

Project outcomes (contract delivery)

Careful evaluation over ten years has provided ample evidence that independent study based on a well-defined learning contract has delivered a wide range of positive outcomes. In academic terms the level of success has been very creditable, with outstanding achievements from many students who were motivated by the opportunity of independent study to work at a level which they might otherwise have failed to achieve. The vocational outcomes have been well-proven with an average unemployment rate among graduates from the course of less than 5 per cent over the last eight years. In relation to service to the community, outcomes are similarly positive with students on the course and graduates from the course working in a wide range of community contexts. Recent examples include contracts on Young Women's Housing Needs completed with the Potteries Young Homelessness Project, Adapting to Blindness completed in association with Warwickshire Association for the Blind and Screening for Coronary Heart Disease with Staffordshire Family Practitioner Committee, North Staffordshire Area Health Authority. In terms of personal outcomes the course has provided remarkable opportunities for students to work towards and achieve a redirection of their life and career. Most courses offer testimonials to students but for the BA (Hons) Applied Social Studies (by Independent Study) the process is frequently reversed by the receipt of glowing unsolicited testimonials from students.

In terms of the elusive goal of 'value-added', the record of the course has been exceptional. It has ceased to be remarkable when a mature student admitted without A levels achieves an upper second classification or above. The example of a student entering with two E grades at A level (and a fundamental lack of confidence in their academic ability) who went on to achieve a first class honours degree (and an immediate contract to publish her independent project on the Psychology of Adjustment to Blindness in Maturity) remains one which the course team will savour. A traditional course would have been most unlikely to deliver such benefits. Finally, the outcomes are positive in relation to ongoing employment. A number of students have successfully completed independent projects based on their current occupation. Thus, a community-based nurse conducting a cardiac survey registered her work and supporting studies for the degree and achieved a first class classification. Another nurse who had followed the course on a part-time basis was expected by her employers to withdraw when given responsibility for the implementation of quality circles in her hospital.

Through the mechanisms of the course, this project and related studies were registered for the degree, leading to another successful outcome. Such examples demonstrate the effectiveness of independent study in encouraging the integration of knowledge and application.

Conclusion

The experience of the course over ten years has demonstrated that when learning contracts are correctly understood and implemented they can offer very considerable benefits to academic staff, students and the wider community. Correct implementation requires a clear understanding that learning contracts should only be entered into by people who have developed the awareness and competence to grasp what is both explicit and implicit in such contracts and also the ability to deliver at the appropriate level. It is also necessary to establish and apply rigorous procedures in the development, agreement, support, appraisal and delivery of the contracts. Through implementing these principles, the course has demonstrated that the ideal of Higher Education for Capability can be a reality.

References

Popper, K R (1965) *Conjectures and Refutations*, London: Routledge and Kegan Paul.

Chapter Five

Negotiating in an Institutional Context

Dave O'Reilly

Since 1974, several thousand students at the University of East London (UEL) have used learning contracts to negotiate individual programmes of study leading to undergraduate and postgraduate awards accredited by the Council for National Academic Awards (CNAA).

As we reflect on some of the critical issues raised by the use of learning contracts for independent study, it is perhaps worth remembering the distinctive features of the UEL experience:

a) that it has been a cross-institutional endeavour, not confined to one Faculty or one course;
b) that the student devises the whole programme of study: it is not a matter of choosing from a menu of modules, nor of doing a pre-set course by distance learning;
c) that the student intake has been predominantly mature and non-traditional in terms of social background and (lack of) educational qualifications.

In its beginnings, independent study at UEL (then North East London Polytechnic, [NELP]) was an innovative response to the introduction of a new qualification, the Diploma in Higher Education (DipHE). Nationally, the DipHE was envisaged as offering a general education with some specialist elements, either as an award in its own right or as a vehicle for entry to teacher training or a specialist degree course. At NELP it was taken further, as an opportunity to create an alternative to the university-dominated model of academic courses which would be more appropriate to the needs of the community in which the Polytechnic was situated – in East End boroughs with some of the lowest take-up rates of higher education in the country. As a planning paper for the DipHE put it in 1972:

> An important principle of NELP policy is to design courses to cater for the needs of prospective students rather than to seek students to fit the courses that NELP would like to run. (Quoted in Robbins, 1988, p. 49)

The project of independent study was thus inextricably linked to the whole question of what the instituition was about – educationally, socially and, indeed, politically. It is not surprising that the subsequent history is both turbulent and complex.

In this chapter, I would like to reflect on a few key issues – to do with the organisation and resourcing of independent study in the University; the type of learning contract we use; the educational models which staff have brought to independent study; and the experience of different types of student. I shall aim to be brief and provocative, but to give some sense of the tensions leading to a radical reorganisation of independent study in the University over the last year. I offer a personal view, not an official history.

Issues of organisation and resources

Independent Study was conceived originally as an integral part of educational provision in the institution. We might illustrate this as in Figure 5.1 (a). The small circle represents the School for Independent Study (SIS), which was established as a central unit to foster the development of independent study throughout the University and to provide central support for student programmes.

From the start, the proposed model had to compete with a perceived model, illustrated in Figure 5.1 (b), which saw SIS as somehow separate from the rest of the University. Whether (b) is an accurate picture is less important than the fact that it was shared by a significant number of colleagues both in SIS and in the rest of the University. It probably did not help that for much of its existence SIS was located in a satellite building of the University some distance from the main teaching sites.

Two key issues here, then, are:

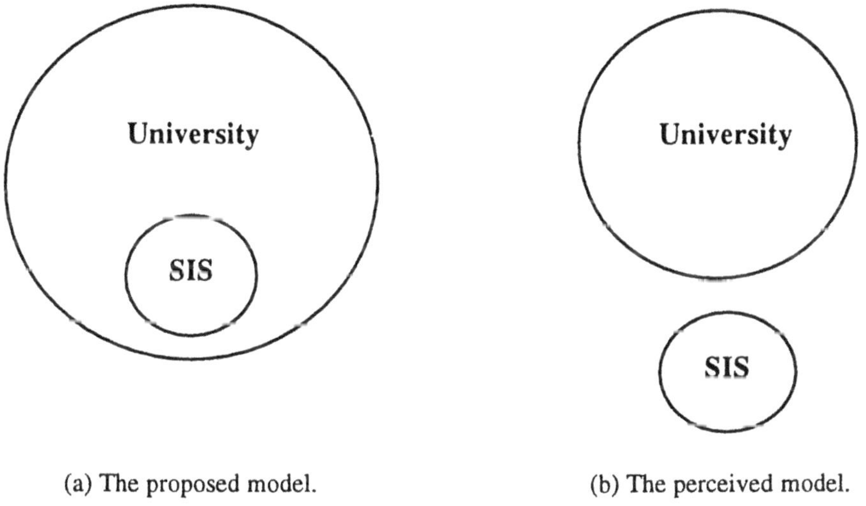

Figure 5.1 *The organisation of independent study in the University*

a) the importance of establishing joint ownership or partnership, and embodying that in organisational arrangements;
b) the dangers of marginalisation of an innovation.

In institutional politics, the issue of ownership is closely linked to the issue of resources. Despite strenuous efforts by the Head of SIS in the 1980s to establish an economy where resources followed students around the institution, a transparent system of accounting was never achieved. Where departments did take independent study students, there was a more or less acute suspicion they were not being properly paid for the supervision and resources they provided. So long as independent study could run on marginal costs, soaking up 'spare' resources, the situation was more or less tolerated, but as it grew to become about 10 per cent of the total student population at the end of the 1980s, and as departments were under greater pressure on their resourcing, it became increasingly difficult to obtain access for students to specialist supervisors and resources. For a mode of study which depends on the notion of the institution as an open resource for learning, this was a serious problem.

The type of learning contract

The method chosen to enable students to construct programmes of study related to their own needs and interests was the learning contract. At various times, contracts have been called statements, proposals of study, learning plans and even, for a short while, learning contracts.

Because students are writing a programme for one or two years, the learning contracts are quite substantial, averaging 15 to 20 pages. The format of contracts differs between different awards, though the sections indicated in Figure 2 give a reasonable idea of their structure.

In Figure 5.2, the first column illustrates the formal language we tend to use as academics. The second column is in plainer language and, though it is less intellectual looking, it helps even MA and MSc students to understand the logical structure of the contract.

1. Relevant prior learning	Where have I been?
2. Present knowledge and skills	Where am I now?
3. Learning aims and objectives	Where do I want to go next?
4. Proposed programme of study	How will I get there?
5. Resource implications	What will I need to help me?
6. Assessment scheme	How will I show I have reached my goals?

Figure 5.2 *Sections of a learning contract of independent study at UEL*

A student typically has one term to write the contract, which means in practice about eight weeks. The drafting and re-drafting are done with support in a central studies tutor group and, where possible, in dialogue with a potential specialist supervisor. The final contract is subject to rigorous scrutiny by external and internal readers who make recommendations to a formally constituted Registration Board which decides whether the contract is acceptable or not. The student has the opportunity halfway through the programme of study formally to register any modifications made to the original contract at what we call the assessment entry point.

For some students, producing the contract can be a burdensome chore; they feel they know what they want to do and just want to get on with it. For others, the contract can become an end in itself, with Section 1 expanding to 30 pages or more. The latter is perhaps more typical of first year students, for whom entry to higher education signals a time of transformation in their lives. The former students may be at a stage of their lives where a more instrumental approach to learning is appropriate. Part of the skill of a central tutor in helping students to write their contract is to recognise and to accommodate quite different expectations of education which learners bring to the institution.

Even trickier is helping the student get to a constructive balance between personal expectations and what the University can offer to meet them (c.f. Weil, 1986). It often helps in such situations if the tutor can offer a model which helps the learner recognise and articulate the process they are going through – what Virginia Griffin has called 'Naming the Processes' (Griffin, 1987).

Three models for independent study

When I first joined the School for Independent Study in 1981, I was surprised, having studied philosophy of science, to find myself in a community of practising Popperians. That is, students were encouraged to think of their learning as analogous to scientific discovery, where the good scientist, according to Karl Popper (1959) proceeds by making bold hypotheses then seeking evidence to refute them. This is a useful model in many ways – it has a strong element of self-criticality built in to it; it offers a reasonable rationale for problem-based learning; and it captures for the learning process some of the allure of scientific method, that great legitimator of knowledge claims. It is possible to consider the learning contract itself as a form of hypothesis, to be tested against the actual outcomes of the learning programme, (though I have to admit I found this a bit far-fetched).

Fairly soon after my arrival at SIS, I discovered a second learning model on offer. This one was derived from humanistic psychology – indeed, from another Carl, in this case Carl Rogers. This model might be typified as student-centred and concerned with education as a process of personal development. Derived from a therapeutic model, the student-centred approach defines a very supportive role for the tutor as a facilitator of learning, though it is not so clear where the critical edge resides.

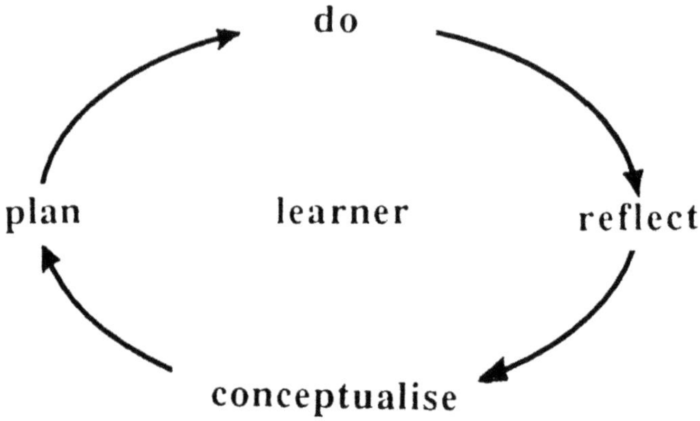

Figure 5.3 *Kolb's experiential learning cycle (adapted from Henry, 1989)*

My own favoured model is based on the experiential learning cycle usually associated with David Kolb (Figure 5.3). Kolb developed a model of learning which goes beyond the purely conceptual domain generally valorised in higher education, and beyond the theory-practice relationship of professional education, to encompass planning and critical reflection as integral phases of a cycle of learning. We can see in this model that for a learner to own the learning fully, he or she should be involved in planning that learning – in the case of independent study, in negotiating the learning contract.

We have also made critical reflection an explicit element of the learning process, requiring each student on the undergraduate programmes to produce a critical review of their learning as part of their assessment. (c.f. Boud, 1988; Mezirow, 1985; Schon, 1987).

However, the broader point to note is how the student's cycle of learning relates to the institutional processes which legitimate it for the award of a Diploma, Degree or Masters, as shown in Figure 5.4.

While I take a fairly pragmatic view of models, seeing advantages and disadvantages with the three I have outlined here, some colleagues take a much more committed line, to the extent that SIS nearly disintegrated several times from the tensions generated between proponents of the different models.

The types of student

Independent Study attracts different types of learner with different expectations and approaches. In a study of past students, John Stephenson (1989) identified six categories of student orientation (Builders of commitment; Takers of qualifications; Searchers of identity; Earners of respect; Provers of

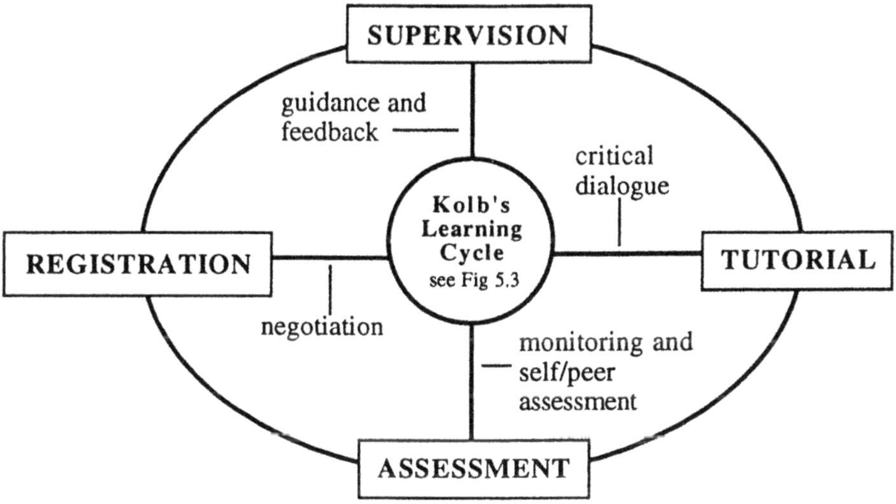

Figure 5.4 *The institutional context of the learning process*

value; Transformers). However, I would like to use a simpler typification to point to different strategies of recruitment with different levels of risk.

One strategy for independent study is to take high-flyers only. These are students that staff generally love to have. It is like having a research assistant. Another strategy is to focus on professional education. In my experience, independent study works particularly well with part-time students working on topics arising from their professional situation. A third strategy is to operate a broad access route for non-traditional students into higher education. This is the route SIS took and, in retrospect, we can see that it was a high-risk strategy.

When it worked, it produced wonderful results. A student who entered the DipHE programme with low self-esteem and a history of educational failure could emerge after three years of critical challenge in a supportive environment with a good honours degree. In current jargon, the process offers a lot of 'value-added'.

However, SIS was carrying too much innovation. We were doing access before the great growth of access in the 1980s; we were doing the Accreditation of Prior Experiential Learning (APEL), for direct entry to our one-year degree before most people (including SIS) had heard of it; we were operating with mature entrants without A-levels long before the University put in place a system of learning support; we were well down the road from norm-referenced assessment for some time before there was a broader debate about criterion-referencing and outcomes of learning.

By 1990, SIS appeared very successful externally, but the tensions between SIS and the rest of the institution, the tensions between different approaches within the School and a rapid catching-up by the world outside together set the scene for a critical report by Her Majesty's Inspectors (HMI) following their visit to the School in November 1990.

Independent study at UEL in the 1990s

The visit by HMI proved to be a catalyst for change in independent study at UEL, with a radical re-organisation of course operation and a re-structuring of the undergraduate programmes. At the same time, the University is embarking on a move towards more flexible delivery of programmes, which entails greater compatibility of independent study with the modular programmes and with the Credit Accumulation and Transfer Scheme (CATS). The key changes for independent study are summarised below.

Reorganisation

We have returned to the original vision, with a small Coordinating Unit for Independent Study (CUIS) and the majority of SIS staff devolved to the six Faculties of the University (Figure 5.5). The intention is to foster ownership of independent study by the Faculties, in order to ensure student access to appropriate specialist supervision and resources.

There are also two College-based licensing arrangements for the undergraduate programme, making eight semi-autonomous course operations in all. I have to say that this produces no more problems than the devolution of the Soviet Union, though on a mercifully smaller scale.

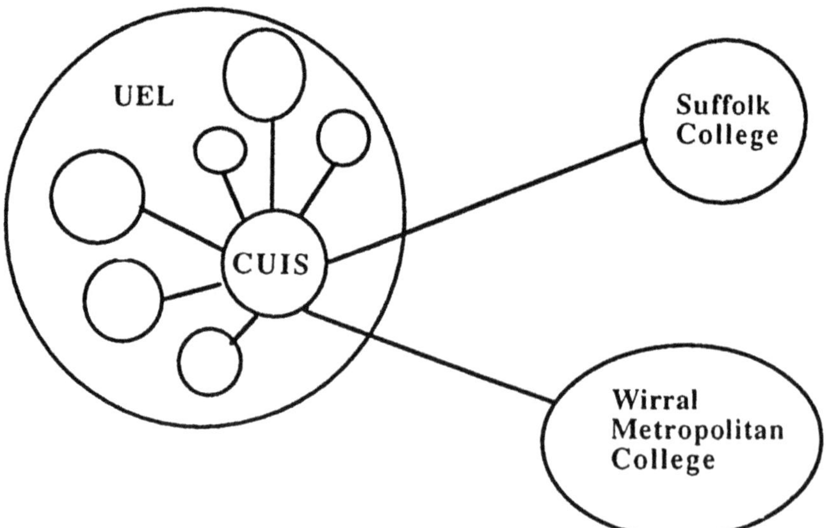

Figure 5.5 *New organisational structure*

Restructuring

Before HMI visited, we were already rationalising the portfolio of DipHE and Degree courses we had developed over the years. In their place we have put a coherent set of staged awards (CertHE, DipHE, Degree/Honours Degree). Additionally we have paid particular attention to tightening up the key quality control points of Admissions, Registration of plans and Assessment, with on-going development of the criteria to guide judgements at each point.

Flexible Delivery

The University is moving towards a more flexible system of programme delivery in which independent study might play a number of roles:

a) as the basis of free-standing awards 'by Independent Study' at undergraduate and postgraduate levels;
b) as a structure for learner-managed learning modules on the proposed extension of the modular scheme, with due emphasis on planning and critical reflection as student learning activities;
c) as a mode of study on any component of any course where student autonomy and reflective practice are to be encouraged;
d) as a means by which students can plan coherent routes of progression through a potentially amorphous and anonymous system of course options. In this scenario, an initial plan could be modified as the student progressed, accumulating a record of achievement which served also as a passport to further study.

Whether all or any of these options blossom under the auspices of a central unit or whether they spring up spontaneously throughout the University in the changing climate of the 1990s remains to be seen. What we may find by the year 2000 is that the use of learning contracts in independent study to date has scarcely scratched the surface of their potential in education.

References

Boud, D (1988) (ed.) *Developing Student Autonomy in Learning*, 2nd ed, London: Kogan Page.
Griffin, V (1987) 'Naming the Processes', in Boud, D and Griffin V (eds) *Appreciating Adults Learning: from the Learners' Perspective*, London: Kogan Page.
Henry, J (1989) 'Meaning and practice in experiential learning', in Warner Weil, S and McGill, I (eds) *Making Sense of Experiential Learning: diversity in theory and practice*, Milton Keynes: SRHE/Open University.
Mezirow, J (1985) 'A critical theory of self-directed learning', in Brookfield, D (ed.) *Self-directed Learning: from theory to practice*, New Directions for Continuing Education No 25, San Francisco, CA: Jossey-Bass.
Popper, K R (1959) *The Logic of Scientific Discovery*, London: Hutchinson and Co.
Robbins D (1988) *The Rise of Independent Study: The politics and philosophy of an educational innovation, 1970–87*, Milton Keynes: SRHE/Open University.
Rogers, C (1983) *Freedom to Learn for the 80's*, Columbus, OH: Charles E Merrill.
Schon, D A (1987) *Educating the Reflective Practitioner*, San Francisco, CA: Jossey-Bass.

Stephenson, J (1989) *'The Student Experience of Independent Study'*, unpublished PhD thesis, University of Sussex.

Weil, S (1986) Non-traditional learners within traditional higher education: discovery and disappointment', *Studies in Higher Education*, **11**, 3, pp. 219–235.

SECTION TWO: LEARNING CONTRACTS AND THE DEVELOPMENT OF SKILLS AND COMPETENCES

Introduction

Mike Laycock and John Stephenson

The Enterprise in Higher Education initiative has raised debate about the design and delivery of the curriculum, the relationship between the curriculum and the world of work and the preparation of people for employment. To a great extent the debate has centred on the kinds of skills students will need to develop. These skills have been identified as 'transferable' and defined as 'generic capabilities which allow people to succeed in a wide range of different tasks and jobs' (Employment Department, 1991, p. 3). The Employment Department (1989) has noted that higher education is responding by recognising that:

> The workplace of today and tomorrow requires employees who are resourceful and flexible and who can adapt quickly to changes in the nature of their skills and knowledge. They will need to be able to innovate, recognise and create opportunities, work in a team, take risks and respond to challenges, communicate effectively and be computer literate. (p. 3)

Similarly, the RSA (1987) has drawn attention to the 'imbalance' between education and training and that the emphasis of traditional education on the acquisition and recording of specialist knowledge is insufficient if:

> 'the vast majority of people go on to live practical lives, making, doing, organising, dealing with problems and doing all this in co-operation with others' (p. 16).

Contributors to this section have applied the learning contract as a means by which students can develop and assess their skills and competences and, in doing so, have emphasised the importance of such skills in the process of learning.

In his discussion of 'informal learning contracts' in philosophy seminars, David Gosling argues that by setting out clear objectives relating to specific abilities or competences, students are enabled to establish their role and responsibility in seminar work. Though students are given more responsibility for 'choosing, planning, organising and implementing their own learning activities', the set of learning objectives is presented to students, against which their selection of the content of courses and the organisation of learning activities can be realised. The contracts themselves specify expectations of students, assessment requirements and the roles and responsibilities of staff. Though Gosling admits that the examples are small steps in an otherwise tutor-determined framework, they play an important part in clarifying expectations and encouraging student responsibility.

Ray Binns describes how, at the University of Wolverhampton, learning contracts can be used both for the development of specialist skills as the explicit outcome (in IT) and the development of personal skills through the use of the contract. Following a taught module at level 1, students develop contracts for increasingly complex orders of skill development at levels 2 and 3. Using an Apple Macintosh at level 2, students develop Desktop publishing and Hypertext skills in addition to other 'capability' skills such as time-management and team-working. An example of group work at level 2, with the Cosford Aerospace Museum, is also described. At level 3, students use their IT skills on an IBM PC or mainframe.

The use of learning contracts in assisting managers to focus on skills or management competences are discussed by both Drew and Lawson at the Sheffield Business School, and at the Sunderland Business School by Penny Marrington. The Certificate in Management programme, discussed by Drew and Lawson, has a prescribed, structured presentation of competences for managers and the learning contract sits somewhat 'uneasily' within the course framework. Nevertheless, with a varied intake, a number of support mechanisms: self-managed study time, mentors, a Personal Development Record to encourage 'reflection and action planning', all of which are 'output-oriented', assist in providing more flexible opportunity.

The Management Development Programme at Sunderland Business School employs the learning contract in stage three of the Programme, as a tool 'to aid thinking about, and the analysis of, the self-development process'. It is seen 'to play a major part in sponsoring the development of managerial competence *and* academic rigour'. Marrington enables readers to go through the process of developing their own learning contract.

References

Employment Department Group (1989) *Enterprise in Higher Education: Key Features of the Enterprise in Higher Education Proposals*, Sheffield: EDG.

Employment Department Group (1991) *Enterprise in Higher Education: Key Features of Enterprise in Higher Education*, Sheffield: EDG.

Royal Society of Arts (1987) *The Art of Change: the RSA at Work*, London: RSA.

Chapter Six

Informal Learning Contracts for Skills Development in Seminars

David Gosling

Twenty years ago, Ivan Illich achieved a certain notoriety in educational circles following the publication of *Deschooling Society* in 1971. Much of the book was devoted to criticisms of the mentality of subservience, inferiority and dependency which traditional school learning induced, but in the chapter on 'Learning Webs', Illich claims that:

> We can depend on self-motivated learning instead of employing teachers to bribe or compel the student to find the time and the will to learn; that we can provide the learner with new links to the world instead of continuing to funnel all education programs through the teacher.(p. 73)

The developments described here may be seen as attempting to realise some, at least, of Illich's programme, although not to the extent of literally 'deschooling society', since they occur within the institutionalised context of philosophy courses on the Modern Studies Degree at Staffordshire University. They represent a limited but determined shift in approach to attempt to capture something of the change in attitude and motivation that Illich was advocating.

The context

We have recently begun to introduce learning contracts within the context of a change towards more 'student-centred' learning principles. We have understood student-centred learning to mean giving students more responsibility for choosing, planning, organising and implementing their own learning activities, although normally within an overall curriculum framework established by the tutor in line with the published and validated course.

This shift of approach from traditional tutor dominated teaching methods aims to foster in students:

a) effective learning of course content;
b) the ability to take effective action to achieve a goal;

c) the ability to work effectively in groups;
d) improved communication and presentation skills;
e) a willingness to take responsibility for organising learning activities;
f) a willingness to be innovative;
g) a recognition of the ways in which information technology can improve study techniques and the presentation of ideas; and
h) confidence in their own abilities.

The assumption here is that our courses must not only aim to teach both understanding and skills or abilities, but also encourage the development of certain attitudes in students towards their learning, themselves and their capabilities.

Objectives

These expectations are laid out in sets of objectives which are at three levels:

a) *general* – abilities we would expect any student taking the degree to develop;
b) *subject-specific* – abilities we would expect a student taking this subject to develop; and
c) *course-specific* – abilities we would expect a student taking a particular course to develop.

We publish these objectives at the outset of the year. For example the second year students received an 'Introduction to year two Philosophy Courses' booklet which included the following somewhat daunting list of general objectives; that is, those which are not specific to particular courses which they take, but which we hope they will achieve in the process of taking all their philosophy courses. Students should be able to:

a) articulate ideas in writing or orally, with reasonable precision and care;
b) present an argument in a logical and coherent form;
c) recognise the dynamic relationship between argument and counter-argument, thesis and anti-thesis;
d) appreciate the importance of supporting claims by the use of relevant evidence;
e) appreciate the importance of surveying and studying the existing literature on a topic when engaging in any enquiry;
f) appreciate the importance of being tolerant of others, to allow them to express their ideas, and to treat views in opposition to one's own with respect at least when these views are expressed with the same respect;
g) recognise what is relevant to an issue and to separate out what is not relevant;
h) recognise unspoken assumptions, ideological presuppositions and taken-for-granted beliefs in one's own and others' thinking;

i) appreciate the value of self-criticism and self-analysis in the search for truth;
j) have sufficient confidence to be able to articulate and defend in writing and in speech conclusions at which he or she has arrived;
k) work independently or with others in a self-motivated and conscientious manner;
l) know how to find information and where to go for further advice in researching particular topics;
m) know how to learn effectively and to be flexible in adapting learning patterns to different skills and contexts;
n) recognise the part played by the choice of language, and written or spoken style, in influencing the nature of communication and its impact; and
o) recognise and enter into an analysis of power relationships mediated through perceptions of categories such as gender, race, class, religion, on interpretations and understandings of modern society.

A second year course: organisation of seminars

In order to help students realise these objectives, we have made three important changes; (1) giving students more say in choosing the content of courses; (2) giving students more responsibility for organising and designing their learning activities in the seminar; and (3) requiring more group and co-operative work.

In a variety of different ways on different courses, we have created the space and the opportunity for students to determine the direction of the course by being able to choose seminar and workshop topics, having 'blank' units where students determine the content and in some cases major texts to be studied. This means that the predetermined course content which the tutor controls via lectures, setting essay questions and exam papers, must not be overloaded, and that there is enough time in the programme for students to be able to work independently and in groups to research information, plan and prepare presentations, identify problems and test solutions.

Second, by encouraging students to think about the whole seminar as their responsibility they begin to think about what sort of activities they would value and to try them out with the group. Part of this change in approach is an attempt to raise the standards expected of seminar presentations. In the past, seminar papers have been read by a single member of the group, which not only in effect disenfranchises everyone else, but makes it very difficult to pick out clear points for the group to follow. The result is that the tutor 'picks up the pieces' and often takes over the whole session. We wanted students to think about the manner of communicating their ideas clearly and effectively so that it became a useful experience for all members of the group. All students on this degree are now given some training in making presentations, using OHPs, producing OHP transparencies and producing hand-outs using word-processors.

Third, we wanted to shift from students seeing their work always as an individual task and to encourage more group and cooperative learning.

Some problems encountered

Some of the problems we have encountered are as follows:

a) student resistance: students exhibit varying degrees of willingness to take up the challenge and produce seminar/workshop presentations of sufficient quality to meet the expectations of the other members of the class;
b) role of the tutor: both students and tutor have to adjust to the different role that the tutor must take, since both tend to fall into traditional expectations that the tutor will lead the discussion, make key decisions, and control student activities; and
c) confusion over expectations: students are often not sure what is expected of them in this new situation. They will therefore tend to revert to methods of presentation with which they are familiar and which give security – such as reading a seminar paper.

Informal learning contracts

In order to try to tackle some of these problems we decided to introduce a contract which would specify both student and tutor responsibilities. The contract would be 'informal' in the sense there was no attempt to require individual students to 'sign' the contract nor was there any specification of sanctions against individuals which went beyond already existing procedures (for example, reporting persistent absentees to the year tutor). It was agreed that the contract should cover the following:

a) expectations about student attendance at seminars and the form of seminar presentations;
b) assessment requirements and criteria for awarding marks; and
c) tutor's role and responsibilities.

The process for negotiating the contract was as follows; the students discussed informally the purpose of the contract and suggested points for inclusion; the tutor drafted the contract and submitted it to the group for amendments; the agreed draft was approved. The agreed contract is provided as Appendix 1.

I would like to draw attention to some of the features of the contract.

a) Given that higher expectations were being placed on students for the quality of their seminar presentations and that they were expected to spend more time working independently, it was agreed that minimum seminar attendance would be set at 50 per cent, but that students should not miss more than two consecutive seminars to ensure that they stayed in touch with the course. No further specifications were made in order to free students to make their own choices about which topics they wished to attend. To enable them to make this choice, once students had chosen their topics a full programme was published and issued to all students with names of seminar presenters and topics to be covered.

b) The 'regulations' regarding the form of the seminar presentations were set by the tutor, but agreed by the group. In this section, expectations about timing, provision of handouts, use of the OHP and the requirement that students should *not* read a seminar paper, were specified.

c) Since assessing oral presentations was a new departure for both staff and students, it was agreed that students could choose whether to have their presentation formally assessed. However, new regulations will require assessment of oral work from next year.

d) The specification of the assessment criteria for both essays and seminar presentations was an essential part of the process of clarification, but arguably not strictly 'contractual' since these were set by the tutor rather than negotiated.

e) The tutor's role is defined in the contract as a supporter and facilitator for the groups preparing their presentations, and as a member of the seminar with no special rights of intervention. This tutor confesses that it is difficult to maintain this part of the contract when students look for a more interventionist role, particularly when a seminar runs into difficulties. But, if students can expect to be 'rescued' at the slightest difficulty, then their independence and self-confidence becomes undermined.

The first year constitution

The second example (given as Appendix 2) of a learning contract, where once again the contract has only an informal status, is a 'constitution' agreed by first year students at the beginning of their philosophy course. The group was asked to draw up a set of rules that would govern the way the seminar would be run which were then formally drafted by the tutor and put to the group for approval. The group accepted the constitution as drafted, with one exception – they rejected the idea of a 'referee' to see that the constitution was being met, a role which has therefore remained with the tutor.

Students specified, for example, that everyone should be asked to express a view, that no one should dominate or disrupt the seminar by engaging in 'private' conversations or show lack of respect by insulting, shouting at, or intimidating anyone in the group. Clearly some of these clauses reflect the anxieties of newly arrived students who were nervous of others whom they imagined would be more confident (or less scrupulous) than themselves, but some important objectives concerning respect for others and tolerance of different viewpoints were clearly identified by students rather than imposed by the tutor.

Student response

Students have indicated that they appreciated the clarification about what was expected of them both for written and oral work; they liked having an input into the content of the contract and the opportunity to control the direction of the course. Difficulties still remain in a number of areas:

a) some students remain reluctant to take control over curriculum content. They feel that it is the tutor's role to say what they should be doing;
b) the extent of student use of the word-processors remains uneven and as a result the quality of materials supporting presentations is also variable in quality;
c) some students find that group work has broken down when individuals have not supported group decisions, not turned up for meetings, or not completed work assigned. As a result some presentations remain a series of individual offerings rather than a genuinely co-operative effort;
d) students have mixed feelings about being assessed on their oral performance. Some welcome the increased range of assessment, but others lack self-confidence;
e) students are concerned that they will not be able to meet all the demands made of them if this style of learning becomes more popular across many courses. There is a need to help students improve their self-management skills, but also for coordination among tutors to prevent overloading on students;
f) students are concerned that tutors should be available to give advice and support in the planning and preparation stage. On the other hand, with higher student-staff ratios tutors can find themselves over-stretched. Clear limits to the demands students can make on the tutor and clear specifications of tutor availability, need to be established.

Conclusion

The examples given here were part of a more general change of perception of the tutor's role and the responsibilities given to students. They are small steps within the framework of a syllabus and assessment procedures which remain largely tutor-defined. Nevertheless, they both have an important place in clarifying expectations of students and tutor, and placing responsibility for parts of the learning process more clearly with the students.

References

Illich, I (1971) *De-Schooling Society*, London: Calder & Boyars.

Appendix 1

BMS2 Philosophy. Persons and Values
Learning and Assessment Contract
The Students' Responsibilities

1. To attend at least 50 per cent of the seminars in each term (unless prevented by illness or other similar good reason) and to arrive in good time. If *more* than two seminars are missed consecutively you will contact the tutor (or the year tutor) to explain the circumstances. If you know in advance that you will not be able to attend a seminar when you are responsible for organising it, you will (if at all possible) notify the tutor before the day of the seminar.

2. To take responsibility for organising the seminar on designated weeks either in cooperation with one or two other members of the group or on your own.

When it is your turn to organise the seminar, you are expected to:

a) meet with the other student(s) organising the seminar, decide on how you are going to approach the topic and agree on duties and roles of each person doing the presentation. For example, who will speak first, whether you will all do your presentations at the beginning or at intervals during the seminar;
b) decide what you want the focus of interest to be, and what you want the other students to do (eg, form discussion groups, answer questions, fill in questionnaires, etc.);
c) do the necessary research to be able to talk for a few minutes on your topic (a maximum of 10 minutes for each person). Try to avoid over-dependence on notes and DO NOT READ OUT A SEMINAR PAPER. Concentrate on communicating what you think are the key points you want to make and to initiate discussion with the remainder of the seminar group;
d) use the blackboard, or OHP if you can (transparencies from me or from Pam Holt in the department's technicians room);
e) provide the group with a short hand-out of notes to accompany your presentation, with references to the sources you have used (using the normal bibliographic conventions).

3. When it is not your turn to organise the seminar, to do sufficient reading in advance of each week's seminar to enable you to participate in discussions and to assist in making the seminar useful and interesting.

4. To fulfil the assessment requirements either by researching and writing two essays, one due at the end of term one and the other at the end of term two; alternatively, electing to replace one essay by being assessed on your seminar presentation. In this case the student reserves the right to have a second essay assessed if he/she wishes.

5. To work within the University's regulations regarding plagiarism.

Assessment criteria

1. The essay(s) will be assessed on the following criteria:

research;	use of argument;
structure;	individuality/originality;
coverage;	written style;
accuracy;	referencing;
critical thinking.	

Not formally assessed but expected:
presentation;
written accuracy (spelling and grammar).

Marks will be awarded on the extent to which the essay:

a) demonstrates evidence of adequate reading/study/research in its preparation;
b) is a structured and systematic answer to the question;
c) addresses the central issues as identified in the lecture programme, lecture notes and your reading of relevant texts;
d) contains accurate representation of the ideas of the authors you have studied;
e) demonstrates critical and analytic skills;
f) incorporates arguments of your own and arguments taken from the literature (properly referenced) to support the conclusion you wish to support, with appropriate discussion of counter-arguments;
g) shows at least that you have arrived at your own individual position with regard to the question or, at best, originality, imagination and flair for the subject;
h) is written in an appropriate style which reads fluently, communicates ideas clearly and avoids ambiguities and confusions; and
i) contains (1), a bibliography with a full set of references to the sources used and (2), footnotes identifying the source and page number for quotations and paraphrases of author's words.

Note: although marks are not awarded for presentation, the essay should preferably be word-processed or typed or if handwritten be clearly legible. Essays should also demonstrate good use of English with accurate spelling and correct grammar.

If a student elects to be assessed on the **seminar presentation** and organisation then the following criteria will be used:

Content
grasp of philosophical content;
range and difficulty of content;
relevance of material chosen;
logical ordering of ideas;
identification of key points;
Communication Skills
fluency of delivery;
clarity of communication;
ability to generate debate;
Materials
referencing of sources;
use of supporting visual aids;
use of handout for the other students in the group.

Note: Modern Studies regulations apply (for example, relating to the penalties for late work). Seminar presentations which are being assessed will be audio-recorded for second marking/external moderation purposes. Students may opt for peer-group assessment to be taken into account. Final responsibility, however, for awarding the mark lies with the tutor.

The Tutor's Responsibilities
I undertake to:

1. give a lecture each week according to the published programme (unless where a reading week has been agreed) which will introduce students to the topic, address the central issues of the topic, and suggest lines of argument for students to consider critically in their own study;
2. provide bibliographies for each topic and, normally, some notes to accompany the lecture;
3. arrive at the seminar every week (unless prevented by illness or other similar good reason) and in good time. If I know in advance that I will not be able to attend I will notify the members of the group before the day of the seminar;
4. participate in the seminars as a member of the group, but only to interrupt the students organising the seminar when I feel there is a danger of the seminar group being seriously misled or given false information;
5. give support to groups preparing seminar presentations by providing recommended texts, assisting with photocopying, and advising on presentation techniques;
6. be ready to answer questions of clarification and explanation to the best of my ability on any matters relating to the syllabus;
7. mark and comment on essays or any other written work (such as mock exam answers) within two weeks of receiving the work, or (where essays are handed in at the end of term) within two weeks of the beginning of the next term;
8. hold individual seminars with students when requested in advance by the student (up to a maximum of three per student of a maximum of one hour each);
9. be ready to offer advice on examination techniques to assist students to prepare in the best way possible for the final examination;
10. report to the year tutor where students have been absent for more than two weeks without explanation and, if there are any other grounds for concern about a student's progress to request a tutorial before passing on further information to the year tutor.

Appendix 2

First Year Seminar Group Constitution

All members of the seminar group will:

a) arrive at the seminar room in good time;
b) do the preparation set out for particular seminars;
c) express a viewpoint on the problem for discussion in the seminar;
d) be prepared to back up their viewpoints with reasoned arguments;
e) be prepared to show an awareness of possible counter-arguments against their viewpoints;
f) listen to the viewpoints of other members of the group;
g) be prepared to answer questions put to them by other members of the group concerning their position;
h) show respect for other members of the group and their viewpoints (eg, no member of the group will insult, shout at, or attempt to intimidate any other member of the group);
i) will be given the opportunity to express their viewpoint in the seminar.

No member of the group will:

a) unnecessarily dominate the discussion;
b) unnecessarily disrupt the discussion: eg, by unnecessarily changing the subject under discussion; engaging in 'private' conversation while discussion is taking place.

The seminar tutor shall ensure that:

a) the membership of small discussion groups is varied from week to week;
b) reading materials are made available at least a week in advance of the relevant seminar.

A 'referee' shall be appointed each week to ensure that the constitution is respected.

Chapter Seven

Development of Capability, DTP and Hypertext Skills Using Learning Contracts

Ray Binns

In 1988, under the auspices of the Enterprise in Higher Education initiative, the University of Wolverhampton provided funds for a new type of course designed to allow students to take responsibility for their own learning and at the same time form links with industry through projects. The course itself was made up of five units (modules), was embedded in the University's Modular Degree scheme and, on successful completion, counted as a Minor in Information Technology.

The course aims were to increase students' understanding of both Information Technology and capability skills. The learning outcomes were that, at the end of the course, the student should be able to use efficiently a variety of software packages such as word processing, Desktop Publishing, Hypertext and databases and to have developed personal skills such as team-working, managing time, negotiating, setting objectives, peer assessment and forming industrial links.

Each module occupied 150 hours of student work over 15 weeks. The first module was not a learning contract but was a taught module in year 1 and at level 1. Students were given the opportunity to work as part of a group but group assessment was not carried out and the IT skills were developed by means of tutored and structured sessions. Following the first year, students then negotiated the content of two learning contracts in their second year at level 2 and, in year 3, a further two at level 3.

The learning contract was a contract made between the students themselves, an academic tutor and an employer. The contract specified, by negotiation, aims, objectives, work schedule, deadlines to be kept, assessment products and the criteria for grading plus a section for any future alterations.

At level 2, IT skills to be developed were those of Desktop Publishing and Hypertext using an Apple Macintosh. This was done via some demonstrations and mainly learning-by-doing. The major capability skills concentrated on were time-management (including keeping deadlines), negotiating criteria, team working (as an equal partner), peer assessment, overcoming difficulties, communication, self-discipline and the ability to pursue an intangible goal.

At Level 3, a change was made to a computer not of the Apple type. Students had to demonstrate their ability to use IT skills learned on one system on another – for example, skills learned on an Apple system to be used on an IBM PC or mainframe. And, in addition to further developing the above level 2 skills, they had to find their own ideas, make contact with an employer and maintain those employer contacts, and work as an unequal member of a team.

Several employers supported the new course with time and in two cases with software. Apple Computers, the Army Careers Service, the Citizens Advice Bureau, Cosford Aerospace Museum, the Midlands Electricity Board, West Bromwich Health Authority and the University Unit for Industrial and Commercial Collaboration were among those for whom students worked. The students produced DTP leaflets and sales guides, Hypertext guides to premises and databases of local firms and organisations.

As a specific example of the use of learning contracts, one particular contract is described. The contract was level 2 and involved four students – Amanda, Tina, Helen and Diane – who formed a group to produce a product for the Cosford Aerospace Museum in the West Midlands. The employer was the Education Officer, Don Prior, and the tutor was the author, Ray Binns. As a group, the students negotiated with employer and tutor the contents of their learning contract. The employer required a Hypertext system for his Apple Macintosh showing the geography of the layout of the museum so that intending teacher visitors could plan visits for their school children to the museum. He also required some leaflets giving details of the museum.

Amanda agreed to produce the leaflets by DTP techniques; Tina, Helen and Diane shared out the work involved in the Hypertext system – in this instance, Hypercard. Tina produced the general site plan, Helen concentrated on the educational aspects, and Diane produced the exhibits section. Students agreed to be judged on their individual contributions to the process via logbooks which were to be reflective as well as descriptive. They would also assess one another, with the evidence for the grade chosen justified by the specific references to the logbook or product. The breakdown of the assessment percentages was negotiated to be 60 per cent tutor, 30 per cent employer and 10 per cent peer. The grades received by the students at the end of the module were Helen A, Diane and Tina B each and Amanda C. The product they produced was outstanding and is currently in place and being used.

The evaluation of the course was, and still is, done via several sources and performance indicators. These include the tutor's logbook, which details comments about each student during the regular meetings which are held. Also included are the use of student questionnaires (to obtain the student experience) and the grades the students obtained. It was found that the students enjoyed the negotiation and being responsible for their own learning but found that there was a little too much freedom..

Students found the group work difficult but rewarding. The peer assessment was unpopular since it was not appreciated that evidence had to be produced to support a high grade. One student attempted a 'free ride' but was 'brought to earth' by the comments in the logbooks of the other students. The quality of the product was, as expected, very high. One student was outstanding with two others producing excellent work. All students learned about working independently of a tutor and about working in a team. All four reaffirmed their intention to continue with the course in spite of the difficulties associated with finding and making employer links.

So far, on the evidence of the students who have participated in the course, it appears that learning contracts encourage independent working and preparing students for contact with employers. A major difficulty is that of persuading the students that capability skills are as necessary as subject or content. This can be overcome to some extent by lecturers who have gained their students' confidence. Although the course is rather inefficient (from a staff/student ratio point of view) this tutor at least finds the opportunity to practice variety in teaching methods very welcome and it is the intention to use this form of learning in integrative studies.

Chapter Eight

Supporting the Development of Managerial Competences Using Learning Contracts

Sue Drew and Steve Lawson

Introduction

Sheffield Business School is committed to providing development, education and services to managers within public and private sector organisations which reflect the requirements and expectations of individuals and employing organisations. Through its Management Development Programme, Sheffield Business School caters for the needs of managers, presently holding either middle or senior management positions as well as those in junior positions, aspiring to middle and senior management roles.

The Management Development Programme encompasses three stages of development; the Certificate in Management, the Diploma in Management Studies and the MBA, lasting one year, one year and eighteen months, respectively. Each is a nationally recognised postgraduate qualification and may therefore be regarded as a terminal qualification or as a stepping stone to the next stage. Individual managers may then choose to complete as much of the Management Development Programme as they see necessary for their development, or as much as they are capable of.

The 'open access' Certificate, discussed here, has been developed and designed within the framework and directives of Sheffield Business School's overall Certificate in Management. This overall programme has also been used for the joint design and implementation of the Certificate with corporate clients.

Some of the key elements of support for learning activities which have been developed in the Certificate, currently in its first year, include a learning contract, support from peers, and a mentor, and self-assessment and action planning materials. An important feature is the help provided not only for students but also for mentors.

Background to the Certificate in Management

A considerable number of the 200 entrants on to the Certificate are graduates but with little or no business qualifications. Typically aged between 23 and 50, with an average age of 33, they are in employment and all, even those in relatively junior positions, have responsibility for some form of resource. One important aim of the programme, therefore, is to enhance their competence in their *present* roles.

The difficulties of managers attending sessions is well recognised by Sheffield Business School, hence a wide range of attendance modes are offered on the Certificate including one full day per week, the traditional weekly afternoon and evening, weekly evenings only and a series of weekends. Additionally, all students irrespective of mode attend common residential programmes. Each mode of attendance within the Certificate has a maximum of 25 participants and there are eight modes of attendance currently in progress.

Structure and content of the Certificate in Management

Within the overall Certificate Scheme, a particular structure has been established, the key features of which are as follows:

a) the three major competence areas associated with Certificate-level programmes have been sub-divided into seven **units of competence**;
b) each unit of competence has been defined in terms of its related:
- elements of competence;
- objectives;
- performance criteria;

Major Competence Area	Units of competence (modules)	Specialist skills options (participants choose 2 from 4)
Personal Effectiveness	1. Managing Oneself 2. Interpersonal Skills	Data Handling Skills
Management Context	3. The Business Environment 4. The Management Task	Language Skills
Management Functions	5. Managing People 6. Managing Information 7. Managing Operations	Financial Skills Marketing Skills

Figure 8.1 *Outline of the Certificate in Management*

- learning and development activities;
- assessment activities.

Participants are also required to extend their skills development by choosing two major skills options in addition to those developed to the competence level. The outline structure of the Certificate is shown in Figure 8.1

Assessment

Assessment of each student is by the production of a personal portfolio, through which students demonstrate achievement of the competences. During the course, students produce a mixture of individual assignments and group projects. These, together with other materials, for example, logbooks and relevant work experience, form the portfolio. Students, with guidance, structure their own portfolios deciding how to demonstrate the competences and what material to include. For each unit, the student produces a learning contract which outlines the specific areas of competence they feel they need to develop and the learning activities and assessment activities to be undertaken.

Support for students

Each week, built into the timetable is a period of self-managed study; two hours in the first term and one hour in each of terms two and three. The overall purpose of each period is to enable students to structure and manage their own learning and the amount of time allocated represents a key proportion of the whole course, emphasising its importance.

For each mode, the students are grouped into learning sets as it is clear students can benefit substantially from each other through shared learning and support, regarding issues such as the learning contract, portfolio preparation and meeting course requirements. As each learning set comprises around five students, there are usually four/five learning sets per mode.

A mentor is allocated for each mode of attendance and is available during the self-managed study periods to help students draft, prepare and progress their learning contracts, as well as being a key contact who will provide general advice and counselling relating to the course and monitor progress. There are eight mentors on the current Certificate, all with obviously different personal styles, all of whom have attempted to place responsibility firmly on the students for the self-managed study periods. Mentors have usually moved from setting the scene, explaining requirements and facilitating the establishment of learning sets to responding to student requests and being available for consultation.

In addition to the self-managed study time and the availability of a mentor at the start of the Certificate, students were given a Personal Development Record (PDR). This explained the system, listed the competences and performance criteria and provided personal audit sheets to help students identify competences already acquired through work or other experiences.

The PDR also provided weekly record sheets to encourage reflection and action planning, termly summary sheets again for recording learning and action planning which might feed into the portfolio, and also blank learning contract sheets.

Support for mentors

The eight mentors were selected from volunteer staff at the Business School by the course leader who wanted lecturers, particularly interested and experienced in this role, to participate. Support for the mentors is facilitated by a colleague in the Business School with considerable expertise in this area.

Prior to the start of the Certificate the mentors, the course leader, and the author of the Personal Development Record met together with the facilitator initially to clarify the mentors' role, discuss appropriate approaches, identify what the mentors hoped for from this experience, and review the Personal Development Record.

The group has continued to meet regularly during the course to discuss experiences, developments, problems and possible solutions, carry out an ongoing evaluation of the process, discuss policy and provide mutual support and encouragement.

Evaluation to date

A questionnaire was provided to elicit students' views on the programme for the first term as a whole. This, together with perceptions from the mentors and course leader, has given some useful indications as to the effectiveness of the scheme to date. A number of issues have already emerged:

a) the materials in the Personal Development Record were found to be over-long and in future may not be used or may be made more concise with suggested approaches rather than being prescriptive;
b) the learning sets can be very productive when operating well but, where this is not the case, they can be a source of frustration. Methods for helping students decide on 'appropriate' groupings are being considered for next year;
c) the issue of how best to cater both for students wanting autonomy and those wanting more structured support is being addressed;
d) the learning contract currently sits rather uneasily in the whole course structure and work is to be done to make it more personally meaningful to students, given that competences are specified and course work required. The term 'learning contract' was found to be off-putting to students and is likely to be replaced by 'Development agreement'. The level or depth of detail which the contract should cover has been extensively discussed by the mentors;
e) the mentors' support group is seen by them as a very valuable mechanism which should be reinforced and extended.

Summary

Obviously, as the Certificate is in its first year, there are learning issues both for students and mentors. However, it is apparent already that the output-orientated rather than input-driven approach adopted in the Certificate provides students from a wide range of organisations with a greater and more flexible opportunity for developing their management competences. We have also built into the course programme the mechanisms described above to support the achievement of those competences for both the students and their mentors. It is certainly a substantial step forward.

Chapter Nine

The Learning Contract as an Aid to Self-development and Managerial Competences

Penny Marrington

The course: a focus on competences

The Management Development Programme at Sunderland Business School attracts a wide range of managers from many different types of organisation. They are interested in taking advantage of the opportunities and efficiencies presented by a three-stage programme (leading to Certificate, Diploma and Masters awards) which incorporates distance learning, weekly workshops, work-based and employer-mentor assessed assignments, and a strong and guided encouragement to self-development towards specified managerial competences. These are for:

Stage One
command of basic facts;
relevant professional knowledge;
analytical, problem-solving and decision/judgement-making skills;
social skills and abilities;
balanced learning habits and skills;
self-knowledge.

and, for:

Stage Two
efficiency orientation;
continued sensitivity to events;
emotional resilience;
pro-activity;
creativity;
mental agility.

And all, applied appropriately as below, for:

Stage Three
the ability to identify strategic direction and take a corporate view;
planning the future rather than managing the present;
influencing other senior managers;
managing other external relationships;
getting others to act rather than doing it yourself;
operating effectively in different organisational settings and national cultures;
absorbing and recalling quantities of data without losing sight of the main issues.

These competences, based on the Burgoyne and Stuart (1978) model, are the focus for individual objective-setting, assessment and achievement for both the requirements of the Programme and the task and process requirements of the manager at work. Much of the specific content of the Programme is thereby determined by the managers themselves, in collaboration with employers, tutors and their peers. The fixed points and containing structure of the Programme are defined in relation to the processes which it is believed managers need to undergo in order to develop or demonstrate the competences.

The context: student responsibilities and peer support

Within this framework, managers are considered to be responsible for their own learning, gathering necessary resources from within and outside the Programme as they see fit. Of course, in the first instance, a great deal of guidance is given in this. Most people's concept of education places a far greater emphasis on the activity of a 'teacher' and the passivity of the learner than is considered healthy in this Programme and, in the beginning, there are levels of resistance and mistrust to be overcome and confidence to be built. One of the most helpful instruments in this is a recognition by the managers that as a group they possess a great deal of expertise, experience and wisdom, and that they are a rich source of support for each other. In the early stages of the Programme, 'support groups' are constituted and reconstituted (by the managers) with a certain degree of fluidity, depending on perceived needs. In the final stage (Stage Three, leading to the MBA), there is a Programme requirement that each manager be assessed by a peer group with respect to their objective and academic approach to a real strategic exercise for which they have had responsibility in their organisation (the project). The project itself is assessed by employers and tutors. At the same time, each manager must be appraised by a peer group with respect to their self-development, in terms of both process and content. A final hurdle is the requirement that each manager convene a panel within which they have a last opportunity to convince employers, tutors and peers that they are Master Managers. All of the activities associated with the Stage Three assessments are complex interactions of task and process, work-place and academia, objective and subjective, and as such require considerable thought, analysis and planning for achievement. 'Learning sets' are an ideal vehicle for such work. They differ from 'support groups' in that they are constituted (by the managers) with particular regard for factors which would be important in successfully meeting Programme requirements, as well as on the basis of personal allegiances. The learning sets tend to operate with rather more formality than support groups. Agenda are raised which reflect objectives set by individuals and the group, and their need to seek support and monitor progress. Meetings are usually minuted, and the minutes may be used in assessments as evidence. Learning sets network with each other, and thus achieve a cross-fertilisation of ideas, but their most valuable function is to provide a safe environment for each manager, where peer support is sharpened by the open and rigorous feedback necessary for learning, development and growth. In a competence-based programme, the most useful feedback is that which is directly 'personalised' to the recipient, and any real learning is bound to involve the discomfort of new self-awareness and change. For these reasons, the relative security and privacy of the set is essential in encouraging managers to give and receive feedback positively, and to experiment with new ways of doing things.

The Role of Learning Contracts

It might be considered that there are many opportunities within the Management Development Programme to use formal learning contracts – for example, in the specification of each work-based assignment, where managers and employers set task objectives and managers pursue self-development goals, or where managers collectively determine the criteria for assessment for an assignment. However, in practice, it has been found that learning contracts are considered superfluous in all areas except one. They are not needed for work-based assignments because the objectives in the work-place, constrained by the Programme specifications for the assignment, provide sufficient definition of, and logic for, the outcomes to be achieved and the activities chosen. Self-development work undertaken by managers within these assignments is not directly assessed, and need not be made explicit, except that it is observed to have a bearing on the manager's demonstration of the relevant competences.

Only in Stage Three, when explicit self-development objectives must be seen to be met, is there a real value in making a learning contract. The primary use of the contract is as a tool to aid thinking about and analysis of the self-development process. It requires the specific definition of terms such as 'goal', 'objective', 'criteria' and 'evidence' in relation to chosen generic, behavioural competences or attributes. The manager makes the contract with him or herself and with the learning set, and in consultation with the set and any other sources of relevant information. The final contractual document, which also indicates where and how evidence of outcomes will be generated, is invaluable as a framework for the assessment of what could easily be a very indistinct area of learning.

The experience of the Programme to date is that some managers make very serious attempts to analyse and manage their own personal attributes and competences; seeking feedback from colleagues, superiors and subordinates, building models of their own patterns of behaviour, and finding ways of developing or modifying the way in which they do things. Those that do are found to be those managers who are deemed to be most successful by employers' or work-based criteria, and who are also considered to be the most academically sophisticated. As yet we are not able to determine cause and effect, but it is likely that the intellectual processes, and practical investigations, prompted by the use of the self-development learning contract, have a major part to play in sponsoring the development of managerial competence *and* academic rigour.

The contracting process

Readers might like to try the following process for themselves.

What would you like to be better at, particularly within the realm of the aforementioned competences, and assuming you are operating at Stage Three?

How do you know that that is what you want? Have people told you, have you asked them? Is it the most efficient and effective area to tackle? Will you get a good pay-off for the effort you put in? Is it something you feel uncomfortable about (a good indication that work would be profitable)? Perhaps you have a general feeling for what you need to do.

But what *exactly* are your objectives? When you say you want to be 'better at person-management' or you want 'to be able to influence other senior managers', what do you mean? Do you need to break down a general goal into more specific components? To be 'better at person-management' – is that to be better at delegating or a better mentor or a better communicator?

Now that you have defined your objectives, you must also define your criteria for success. What are the characteristics of a 'competent' (or, let us aim high, 'excellent') delegator? What sort of qualities does an 'influential manager' have? There are likely to be many different answers to these questions – which ones are the right ones? You will need to research this. And which are the useful answers? It is probably easier to tackle the 'presenting a clear picture of the situation' aspects of being an influential manager than the 'being tall and charismatic' ones.

Then you will need to convince yourself (and maybe others) that you have achieved your objectives. What evidence would be appropriate? 'I will know that I am an excellent delegator when...' – what? Generally, it would better if the evidence were behavioural, the evidence of your own eyes, ears, feelings. Don't worry if some of this evidence doesn't seem very 'scientific' – learning, in particular, to recognise and trust your own feelings about a situation, is important if your increased managerial competence is to become second nature.

The final component of the contract will be the definition of the activities which you are going to undertake in order to develop and demonstrate increased competence in your chosen area, and a statement of the resources required. Where possible , the activities should be in the mainstream of your work and life, not an artificially created add-on which may have limited validity. You will need to think carefully about where you can find opportunities for your self-development. Most tasks contain processes that could be managed in a variety of ways – do things differently and observe the outcomes. If you need to rehearse a risky activity before launching yourself into the 'real world', then use a learning set.

You will probably want to introduce some 'quality assurance' mechanisms, and the understanding that a contract may be renegotiated if it becomes inappropriate. Some of the pitfalls might be disclosed by the following questions:

Is this going to be worth the effort?
Am I in a position to initiate and/or maintain this?
How far do my results depend on other people?
Is there any possibility that this could be sabotaged – by others – or by myself?
What will things be like when I'm different?

In the Sunderland Business School Management Development Programme, we have found that learning contracts for self-development have been used as:

a) brainteasers to sharpen thinking;
b) maps to encourage steps into the unknown;
c) structures for support; and
d) guidelines for appraisal.

A lot of benefit from a simple tool!

Reference

Burgoyne, J and Stuart, R (1978) *Management Development: context and strategies*, London: Gower Press.

SECTION THREE: LEARNING CONTRACTS AND THE WORLD OF WORK

Introduction

Mike Laycock and John Stephenson

Learning contracts have provided practitioners with the means by which students can systematically engage in experience-based learning. Working in partnership with external clients to gain experience of applying specialist skills and knowledge, of testing the dynamics of that experience and to gain a comprehensive understanding of it is a key feature of both the Enterprise in Higher Education initiative and the Higher Education for Capability scheme.

The considerable concern expressed about the dominant value system in the UK education system, seen as largely irrelevant to the needs and interests of many people, has resulted in strenuous efforts to re-define that value system.

The Enterprise in Higher Education initiative (Employment Department, 1991), for example, has sought to:

> ...bridge the cultural divide between industry and commerce on the one hand and academic education on the other. Some of the failings of the UK economy have long been attributed to the existence of this gulf.
>
> One of the objectives of the EHE programme is to enhance the quality and quantity of contact between people in higher education (both staff and students) and employers. There is the potential for everyone involved, staff, students and employers, to benefit from this exchange – partnership – directly and indirectly. (p. 10)

Whatever the working environment for students there will be a need to innovate, recognise and create opportunities, work in a team and communicate effectively. Developing personal effectiveness so as to enhance confidence, competence and capability can be achieved through a learning process which encourages students to set objectives, to be flexible and to adapt to rapid changes in skills and knowledge. EHE has stressed that enabling students to be lifelong learners and to be better prepared for their working lives is an essential element of the educative process.

It is certainly a change valued by employers. Those companies introducing the concept and practice of Total Quality Management (TQM), for example, value employees who can work autonomously and in teams, review their own performance and take responsibility for their own development.

Though higher education is conscious of the need to address the forging of productive and meaningful links with employers/practitioners, the strategies and tactics to be employed are less clear. Within EHE (Employment Department, 1991), all contracted HEIs are intent on:

> furthering co-operative relationships with a variety of large and small, local and national, public and private and voluntary sector organisations (p. 10) [though] few have tried to formulate a partnership strategy. (p. 14)

This section addresses the ways in which the learning contract is central to the process of formulating partnership strategies and the way in which it can act as the catalyst for achieving the kinds of changes advocated. Contributors have identified a number of contexts in which the learning contract has assisted in formalising the process of linking the curriculum with the world of work in project work, placement and work experience. The learning contract also provides a means of reconciling different objectives. For students, a contract can establish their *ownership of personal and professional objectives*. For higher education institutions, it becomes a means by which concerns of *critical distance* can be established and for employers, issues of *relevance* can be highlighted.

From the perspective of an employer, Graham Spaull articulates the importance of learning contracts or agreements in providing a focus for work experience. They form a tripartite agreement of, and commitment to, objectives with 'real' outcomes in terms of skill development and link work-based learning to assessment which provides evidence of achievement against objectives. He also points to the need for clarity of understanding of the process by which learning contracts are agreed and their outcomes assessed. Educators, students and employers must also be clear about the value of learning contracts in experiential learning.

For the use of learning contracts in 'history project work' with employers, David Nicholls identifies the skills encouraged as 'self-organisation, creativity, meeting deadlines, problem-solving, numeracy, presentational and communication skills, the ability to work with others, analytical and critical abilities, and a better understanding of the structure of the workplace and the ability to adjust to it'. Though he appreciates that the process of contract negotiation can be labour-intensive, a 'simple time-saving device is to keep a contract pro forma as a file in a word-processing program which can be copied to create the outline for each individual contract'. Clarity in negotiation between tutor, student and client will ensure, thereafter, that 'the contract provides them with a clear and readily accessible point of reference' and, for collaborative projects, 'a format which is followed by each contributor to the overall project thus maintaining consistency between its various constituent parts'.

Much wider potential for use, so that students are familiar with the process, is also identified by Nicholls. He sees their application in postgraduate dissertations, student mobility schemes, portfolio development, accrediting prior experiential learning and finally, 'The adoption of contracts for all course units would perhaps lead to more thought being devoted by both teachers and students to questions of coherence and progress, to consideration of the respective contributions of different units towards encouraging a wide range of competences, and to explicit attempts to plug gaps in a student's educational experience'.

Wendy Stewart-David documents the use of learning contracts on the BA (Hons) Business Studies course at Newcastle Business School as a means by which students would 'graduate with ability and motivation to be independent lifelong learners' and 'to stimulate initiative, creativity and innovative thinking'. The course intersperses their use for college-based work and placement experience. She too reiterates the point that students need 'a clear understanding of the educational principles underlying the approach' and familiarity with the importance of a cyclical approach to learning. The problems of assessment are addressed by the clear specification of criteria enabling consistency with 'more traditionally delivered subjects'. For employers, the approach represents a 'sensible, easily understandable and a promising way of encouraging students to be more flexible'. For tutors, two solutions to the issue of resource management are offered; to appoint specialists to facilitate all contract learning and/or to view the work as mainstream academic research.

Enterprise funding supported the development of learning contracts in clinical practice placement on the physiotherapy degree at the University of East London. Jean Hay-Smith identifies the module 'Introduction to Clinical Practice' as the period when students can look at the process of setting and negotiating learning objectives prior to placement. Three areas for objective-setting, related to clinical practice, have been established. Monitoring progress is accomplished through the use of work diaries and peer group reflection. Problems associated with clarity of understanding are addressed in seminar work.

Isabell Hodgson's pilot study indicates that the learning contract is 'seen as a framework for structuring and planning the student's learning experience during the industrial placement' and several workshop sessions are held to brief all parties on the stages, factors and construction of the learning contracts and their evaluation. For students, she points to the importance of the sense of achievement, ownership and motivation and recommendations for their wider use. For employers, the introduction of learning contracts was a success but could be dependent on the motivation and commitment of those involved.

Finally, Iain Marshall and Margaret Mill describe a Training, Enterprise and Education Directorate (TEED) funded project at Napier University which utilises learning contracts as a means by which sandwich students can earn academic credit for their placement experience. Marshall makes clear that the learning contracts are *student-driven,* though subject to negotiation and renegotiation with academic staff and employers. Linking work-based learning to credit has an important function in enabling resources to follow credit and to encourage more commitment from students and employers. The approach focuses on learning outcomes which are job- and course-related and associated with personal development. Marshall is clear that the focus will enable a shift in thinking away from time-based units of credit towards credit for learning outcomes, thereby providing the formal acknowledgement of work-based learning. The model is taken one stage further, targeting employees in small businesses who may use learning contracts to determine training needs and to access resources in higher education as a means of meeting those needs. The work also demonstrates the value of contact with large companies in providing a conduit to their smaller suppliers. It is a small example of the work undertaken with employees, which is the subject of the final section.

References

Employment Department Group (1991) *Enterprise in Higher Education: Key Features of Enterprise in Higher Education,* Sheffield: EDG.

Chapter Ten

The Employer's Perspective

Graham Spaull

Why learning agreements?

When considering why learning agreements should be used within Rover, it is perhaps necessary to go back over recent years and examine briefly some events that have taken place to ensure Rover is more competitive with other vehicle manufacturers.

In the period 1979 to 1985 both the Rover Cars and Land Rover parts of Rover Group carried out major changes in facilities and raised productivity and quality levels significantly. However, it remained clear that this progress was still insufficient to match the standards of the Japanese automotive companies and the company had inadequate financial returns due to its high cost-base. Problems were very much related to management style and company culture. Traditional UK industry has spent decades taking responsibility away from first-line managers which has resulted in slow decision-making and an absence of leadership. It was believed that the essence of good management was to get ideas out of the heads of bosses and into the hands of labour, whereas the core of management should be precisely the art of drawing on the combined brainpower of all its employees in the service of the business.

Rover Group introduced a Total Quality Improvement programme (TQI) in 1987 which had the objective of involving the whole workforce in the quality of everything that is done on a day-to-day basis. This initiative was cascaded through the organisation at every level with five main requirements in mind. These were:-

a) *leadership from the top* – not just the Chief Executive, but every person in charge at every point in the organisation;
b) *effective management of the cost of quality* – not just drawing what the cost is, but using it to drive waste out of the organisation;
c) *a focus on customer satisfaction* – primarily on the external customer but with the understanding that this can only be done by satisfying internal customers as well;
d) *continuous improvement;*

e) *everyone involved.*

These principles challenged many traditional approaches. A major project was born from the application of these principles which was known as 'Success Through People'. One aspect of this project has been to look at a work-experience scheme for undergraduates that has been operating within the company for some years, to improve its effectiveness.

Implications for undergraduate placement and recruitment

Rover no longer offer full sponsorship for a degree course but have introduced a Student Placement Scheme which gives undergraduates the opportunity of a placement of up to six months in the penultimate year of the degree course. As a result of this Scheme, an increasing number of graduate recruits (from 8 per cent in 1989 to a target figure of 60 per cent in 1992) have had previous work experience with the company. Although placements in past years had been encouraged, their success was somewhat patchy as they depended heavily on the line manager's ability to find meaningful work for students. Experience proved that there was a need for any students of placement to have a specific focus, thus giving commitment from the student, the line manager and the tutor to an agreed set of objectives which were realistic and achievable. Without this direction, it was difficult to assess an individual objectively and invariably meant that mundane tasks were given, creating demotivation for the students. Real work comes high on the list of priorities for most students and they are usually keen to feel they are contributing to the company effort. It is a requirement to ensure, whenever possible, that this can be achieved even when it is a simple task. Linking education to work is now, at last, seen to be a key part of the education process and it has been shown that it is no longer satisfactory to churn out graduates who are narrow in their education and learning. The culture change within Rover is demanding that personal transferable skills and business skills are vital for successful operation within the company. Therefore, these need to be an integral part of the learning process through higher education.

Learning agreements: a pilot scheme

To address these points, learning agreements were introduced with a pilot group of students from various disciplines at Coventry University. Learning agreements had been previously used as part of a management programme and had proved to be successful in giving the focus that was required. This was a further opportunity to exploit the potential benefits that could be gained from their use.

The pilot scheme was conducted during the summer vacation period of 1991 in conjunction with Coventry University through a Training, Enterprise and Education Directorate (TEED) funded extension project on learning agreements. Twelve students were selected, using psychometric tests and interviews and, whenever possible, placements were matched with student requirements. Learning agreements, identifying the objectives to be achieved during the placement period and the resources that were necessary to achieve these objectives, were established for all the students. To link the learning gained during the placement, a method of assessment was established to provide evidence of the achievement of the objectives. This assessment formed part of the student's overall course assessment. The agreement was then signed by the student, line manager and tutor. A process was created which allowed the agreement to be redefined during the placement period, reflecting the true circumstances experienced during the placement.

A review of the pilot

Mid-term and final reviews were conducted to identify the extent to which the students were being enabled to develop a meaningful agreement and to what degree they were being supported towards the achievement of the goals set out in the agreement.

The major finding from the review was that students took on responsibility for their own learning. It has motivated the students, not only in the workplace, but also when they get back to university. It is real work with parameters. Students feel that they want to contribute and certainly our impression has been that by the use of learning agreements, they feel that they are achieving this. They are actually doing something real, it is useful, and they can see the results of it.

Learning agreements have assisted the development of personal transferable skills. One of the criticisms of graduates is that they cannot write a report in the sort of terms that we want, that they have difficulty in basic presentations, and so on. The development of business skills is also critical. Sixty-five per cent of our graduate intake are actually engineers and it is vital that business skills as well as engineering skills are an inclusive part of the learning agreement.

With learning agreements there is a focus for work experience. A lot of work experience in the past has been wasted, either because it was irrelevant, or students were given menial tasks to do. Since objectives are actually written down, we have something to measure straight away. There is commitment to agreed objectives by the students, the tutor and the manager. This creates a tripartite agreement involving all parties and ensures there is a clear understanding of what will actually happen during the placement period. In conjunction with the University, we looked at what takes place during the placement period and, wherever possible, we have been able to start to accredit the work.

There were also some negative comments, as those involved were encouraged to criticise the scheme. The notion of a learning agreement was not central in the perception of most of the students, managers or tutors. It was commented that the learning agreement as a device was less important than the opportunity which was being given to the student to develop the sort of transferable skills which would be useful in an employment context.

There was some difficulty over the creation of realistic learning objectives. Students were not aware of the opportunities that were available to them prior to the commencement of the placement and, although an open forum meeting took place between all three parties, it proved difficult to agree on what was to be achieved in this environment.

The process of negotiating learning agreements was not one with which the students were generally familiar. This is a problem to be addressed within the higher education system generally. It was suggested by several managers that the students should be involved in a two-part process in which the first placement is purely exploratory, giving them the opportunity to investigate the possible linkages between course objectives and learning opportunities within the company. This would then inform their negotiation of the learning agreement for the second placement. This is an interesting variation of the dedicated placement, laying the ownership of the learning objectives very clearly at the door of the individual student.

Work dominated the learning agreements, not giving time to address the objectives. For the agreement to play a significant role, it is vital that it is central to the placement and that a regular review against its objectives is conducted. In general, the students' perceptions of the benefit of the scheme were a direct consequence of the 'employment as a target' motivation. They saw it as giving them useful experience of the world of work and helping them to confirm their career choices.

It was apparent that in many cases the students were expecting managers to lead them by the hand; they were significantly lacking in the experience of determining and planning for their own learning needs. Managers were happy to provide what they have traditionally provided but were not always aware that this should have been a more individually tailored experience. Where the manager and student were aware, the scheme was delivering what appeared to be high quality individualised programmes of learning and the potential for academic credit was greatly enhanced.

One of the aims of the learning agreement was to accredit learning obtained during the placement period towards the individual's course. However, it was only in a minority of cases that specific credit against the degree course was actually given. If it did not fit into the existing syllabus then the products of the learning agreement were seen as 'add-on' rather than being integrated into the course. The project work to be undertaken in the last year of the course was seen to be the common link.

Tutor support proved to be inconsistent during the placement period. There were varying degrees of belief in the process, and visits during the placement period varied accordingly. There is considerable difficulty in ensuring personal visits take place regularly during a vacation period, so this aspect of support needs careful review to ensure support is maintained with minimum effort.

Conclusion

The pilot scheme has enabled a study to take place which has given indications of the benefits of such a scheme. In essence, it has proved that the main difficulty in obtaining these benefits has been due to ignorance of the scheme prior to its commencement. Although extensive communication was given, it seems necessary for all parties to have had a meaningful experience, and then to build on this for the future. The lessons learnt from the 1991 pilot scheme are to be incorporated in future applications of learning agreements. In 1992 the approach is being developed further, with learning agreements being used with student groups at the University of Hertfordshire, the University of Birmingham and again at Coventry University.

It is only through continual cooperation and working together, that an initiative of this nature will prove to deliver its full potential.

Chapter Eleven

Using Contracts in Project Placements

David Nicholls

Introduction

'Independent Study in History'[1] is a third-year option offered to students taking the BA Historical Studies and the BA Humanities/Social Studies degrees at Manchester Metropolitan University. The course unit was devised with two central objectives in mind – to allow students to *apply* skills acquired during their undergraduate programme to practical topics encountered in an environment outside academia, and to *extend* their educational experience by emphasising new skills that would be required in these practical situations. By allowing students to gain work experience in a non-academic environment, *though one appropriate to their historical training*, 'Independent Study' sought to augment their range of competences and thus help prepare them for later employment.

Among the skills identified as likely to be encouraged by 'Independent Study' were self-organisation, creativity, meeting deadlines, problem-solving, numeracy, presentational and communication skills, the ability to work with others, analytical and critical abilities, and a better understanding of the structure of the workplace and the ability to adjust to it. Students would have acquired some of these skills already, but 'Independent Study' would oblige them to put them to use outside the classroom. Above all, placement with an external client would mean that students would have to take a much more active control over their own learning experience, often working on their own, setting their own goals, responding to problems as they arose, and working in conditions that would approximate to those that they might expect to experience upon graduation. In this way, they would need to mobilise new skills in response to the new circumstances in which they now found themselves. By going beyond teaching for certain specified objectives, therefore, 'Independent Study' set out to empower students. It provided them with the circumstances and opportunities in which they would have to learn for themselves, and in which they would come to take greater responsibility for their self-development and for their professional relationship with other people.

Independent study in history

In terms of its operation, 'Independent Study in History' began in 1989 and over 30 students have taken the course unit to date (1992). Students are normally expected to spend a half-day per week with an external client for the approximately 24 weeks of the autumn and spring terms (October to Easter). The organisations with which students have so far been placed can be categorised into three broad types: commercial and industrial enterprises, libraries and museums, and community organisations.

Learning contracts are negotiated between client, student and tutor during the early weeks of the autumn term, and these spell out the scope of the projects and the manner in which they will be assessed. Despite variations in the contracts, assessment has normally taken the form of a short (approximately 1,000 words) interim progress report, and the final product(s) of the project. Examples of such final products have included market surveys and reports, computer software, historical information packs, catalogues of historical records and archives, historical publicity material for companies, historical research for clients, the organisation of museum and library displays, articles for company journals or newsletters, historical material on video or cassette, and historical guides. A project can include more than one product. Collaborative projects are possible and certain of the projects were perceived from the outset as long-term, with a view to other students continuing with them in subsequent years.

The clients play an integral role in the assessment of their particular students and are assisted with written and verbal guidance. The students, for their part, negotiate the weighting and distribution of marks across the various elements that make up their projects and are encouraged to discuss the evaluations of their work at each stage of the assessment. Student learning and the progress of the course unit are monitored and evaluated by means of questionnaires to clients and to the students themselves. Comments on the unit by both clients and students have, on the whole, been very favourable. Indeed, part of the success of Independent Study can be gauged from the quite considerable use that the clients have made of the students' work.

The role of the learning contract

Having briefly described the operation of Independent Study in History, the remainder of this chapter will concentrate upon the role within the course unit of the learning contract. The first point to stress is that the contracts are not complex documents. Indeed, there is virtue in confining them to the most basic and essential data – such as the student's name, course, an outline of the project, and details on the manner in which the project will be assessed. The period at the outset of the course unit when the contracts are negotiated is a labour intensive one for the tutor. It is important, therefore, to make the process as straightforward and as manageable as possible. One simple time-saving device is to keep a contract *pro-forma* as a file in a word-processing program which can be copied to create the outline for each individual contract, and into which the specific details can then be inserted. Moreover, one of the great advantages of the learning contract is that its terms can be modified to match the appropriate requirements of the individual students. For example, additional details can be incorporated on such points as anticipated costs, the availability of resources and support systems (such as books, videos, access to word-processors), special needs (such as training in handling databases) and so on. The following is an example of a contract that has been used in Independent Study in History, but with the names of the student and client omitted in order to respect their anonymity.

HISTORY: INDEPENDENT STUDY CONTRACT (1991–2)
Name
Course: Humanities/Social Studies
Mode (Course unit or Diss.): Dissertation

Outline of Project
1. To organise and catalogue the Lees Papers held in Oldham Local Studies Library – the catalogue to be produced in printed and in disk forms.
2. To put on an exhibition making use of the papers and of other artefacts found during the cataloguing.
3. To write an historical essay on one aspect of the activities of Sarah Lees (the precise topic to be identified at a later stage), that will serve as a source of information for the library and for future researchers into her life and work.

Method of Assessment
(Note – copies of all pieces of work for assessment should be submitted to the client as well as the tutor.)
1. An interim progress report of approx. 1,000 words to be submitted on 4 Dec.1991 – 20%
2. The catalogue, to be submitted in printed and disk forms, by 25 March 1992 – 15%
3. The exhibition at Oldham library to be mounted towards the end of the Spring Term – 15%
4. The final project of approx. 3,000 words to be submitted by 25 March 1992 – 50%.

Possible Costs
Travel costs to Oldham – to be negotiated with the Enterprise Office

Meetings
Progress Report meetings will be held in Room 4 at the following times:
Wed. 4 Dec.1991 in Ormond Rm.4 at 1:30pm
Wed. 25 March 1992 in Ormond Rm.4 at 1:30pm

External Client
Oldham Local Studies Library
Signatures Student Date
Client
Tutor

It is essential to grasp that these are not legalistic documents. The emphasis is upon 'learning' rather than 'contract', the legal connotations of which might prove intimidating to many students. It is incumbent upon the tutor to make this absolutely clear to each student at the outset. Indeed, the negotiation of the contract is perceived as an intrinsic part of the learning process in which the student is encouraged to think carefully about the aims and objectives, skills, organisation and planning integral to the work which they have chosen to undertake. The student is thereby involved in education as a reflective and pro-active process. Following on from this, the Independent Study learning contract is never treated as an inflexible and immutable statement of the student's programme of work. The contract is not intended to be a tablet of stone, and the student should not see it as such. Rather, the contract is open for re-negotiation as the project unfolds. The student is fully apprised of the constraints (deadlines, meetings, obligations to clients, contribution of the unit to the overall assessment, etc.) within which changes will be permitted. But, the contract is intended, in essence, to establish the parameters within which a student's learning experience can be allowed to evolve. The contract is therefore tailored and, if necessary, adjusted at appropriate moments in order to meet the learning needs of the student.

The advantages of using learning contracts

There are very cogent reasons for using contracts in this flexible and constructive manner. Not only does it empower the student but also, by emphasising the facilitation of learning over conventional didactic practice, it compels teachers to review their pedagogic practice and changes the tutor-student relationship. Indeed, a contract is not simply concerned with the obligations of the student. It is also about the obligations of teachers, and it can be used by the student as a basis for appeal against a recalcitrant teacher who, for example, misses a contracted meeting, or fails to return assessed work within an agreed time. In this way, the contract forms the basis for a dialogue of equal parties to the educational process, and makes it a dialectical rather than didactic experience.

Similar points can be made with regard to the relationship between learning contracts and assessment. The overall mark for the course unit is broken down and distributed in very precise ways to the different elements that make up the project. In this way, assessment is used constructively to encourage and reward the development and demonstration of particular skills and competencies, especially those which are under-employed or given little recognition in the more conventional academic programme or its assessment procedures.

From the students' point of view, the contract gives them a much clearer picture of how they are being assessed and, accompanied by a skills profile, of the criteria involved. Experience has shown that, in negotiating the ways in which the various elements of assessment are to be distributed, students are more than willing to accept advice so that a greater weighting is given to those parts of the project that involve the demonstration of a higher order of skills. Indeed, routine tasks such as the cataloguing of records, sometimes take up an amount of time which is disproportionate to their contribution to the overall assessment. Students tend also to devote more attention to presentation. This is partly because presentational skills are explicitly encouraged by Independent Study (training in word-processing is universally available and additional facilities, such as access to desktop publishing programs, have been provided where appropriate), partly because their interest in the project leads them to *want* to present it well, but also, no doubt, because students are conscious that they are working for an employer.

The time expended on project work of this sort has, therefore, to be very carefully monitored. Precise guidelines are made available to both clients and students, but could also be included, if a tutor wished, in the contract itself. Just as they are keen to present their work well, students are likewise inclined to become so engaged in their placements that they spend more time upon them than the recommended requirement. The contract does, however, provide a useful means by which to regulate student progress. It can be used to specify the dates by which a series of stages in the project have to be completed, and it can provide for periodic meetings when progress can be reviewed. Formal meetings of this sort are ones which students are contractually obliged to attend. Of course, they also meet their tutor on numerous 'informal' occasions to discuss progress.

The contract is a particularly important document in relation to external placements. The client, as well as the student, must be clear as to exactly what the project entails, and the respective contributions to be made by the three parties involved. The contract provides a useful summary of these arrangements but is not sufficient in itself. In the case of Independent Study, the tutor provides the client with written and verbal guidance about course objectives, skills profiles, length of placements, assessment norms and procedures, and so on. The client is encouraged to contact the tutor if there are any questions to be resolved. Personal meetings are best of all if they can be arranged. Good tutor-client relations provide the basis for present and future cooperation and, thereby, make the task of placements that much easier. The contract emerges from a lengthy process of tripartite negotiations in which the clients play an essential part, and their signature confirms their approval of its terms and conditions. Thereafter, the contract provides them with a clear and readily accessible point of reference throughout the period of the placement.

This last point about learning contracts – that they are a readily available statement of a student's programme of work – is important in other ways. For example, the existence of a contract makes it much easier for a colleague of either the client or the tutor to step in and maintain a supervisory role during periods of absence through illness or whatever cause. Moreover, contracts are a useful means of informing other tutors of what is going on in terms of educational practice. In this way, they may be alerted to possibilities that had not hitherto occurred to them, and be encouraged toward innovation and experimentation of their own. Finally, the learning contract contains an explicit statement of the aims and objectives of a particular project which can be used, along with the supporting documentation on general course unit objectives and anticipated skills and expectations, as a measure of the success of the unit. With Independent Study, both clients and students are involved in this monitoring process. They are asked to complete questionnaires which seek their judgement of the operation, experience and fulfilment of course objectives in the context of the contracted aims and the skills profiles.

Potential applications of learning contracts

I have focused so far upon the part which learning contracts have played in the operation and management of a specific course-unit – Independent Study in History. Observations on the usefulness of contracts have, however, been couched in a general way so that the reader can consider if they are apposite to their own teaching circumstances. Potential applications for the broader adoption of contracts in relation to project work are not too difficult to imagine. One obvious place where they can be useful is in the conventional undergraduate dissertation. Many courses and disciplines expect students to complete an extended essay or thesis, based upon some independent and original research, as part of the final year of their undergraduate programme. History students at Manchester Metropolitan University are asked to write a dissertation of 8–10,000 words in which, most typically, they are expected to demonstrate an ability to provide a critical, historiographical review of extant secondary materials and/or make analytical and constructive use of primary sources. The author has found that contracts are appropriate here for many of the reasons described in relation to Independent Study – especially the opportunity they give for clarification of content at the outset, the capacity they afford for using assessment constructively (for example, by identifying the proportion of the mark to be assigned to the bibliography, presentation, content and so forth), and the precise statement they offer with regard to the mutual obligations of student and tutor in their striving towards a common educational goal. It is largely for this last reason that the author would recommend the adoption of contracts in relation to postgraduate theses, where the obligations of supervisors can be all too easily neglected or, at best, are not guaranteed. A careful definition of these and other matters relating to the postgraduate tutorial relationship would introduce a greater rigour and, thereby, inject a larger dose of professionalism into what can be very much a lottery system in which constructive guidance is left to the whim of individual tutors.

Contracts are also useful in regard to collaborative projects, where the specific contributions of individual members of the team can be precisely delineated and distinguished. Likewise, they play a vital role in the management of long-term projects passed on from one student to another. In the case of Independent Study placements with Stockport libraries, for example, a long-term project is in progress whereby each year a student produces a guide to the holdings of the libraries which relate to one particular area of the metropolitan borough. The contract provides a format which is followed by each contributor to the overall project, thus maintaining consistency between its various constituent parts.

Wherever there is a process of negotiation between student and tutor, contracts can play a constructive and helpful role. As higher education is broadened and teaching changes – 'more means different' – one important element in managing this change has been, and will continue to be, an enhancement of the role of the teacher as a facilitator. In the age of mass higher education, contracts can help to individualise the learning process and thereby to reassure students and increase their confidence. It is likely, therefore, that the negotiated contract or programme of study will, in these changed circumstances, become more common. Various forms of 'negotiated study' have, for some time now, been pursued by several institutions of higher education. Students are able to negotiate course units or patterns of study that are not directly available upon the degrees for which they are registered. This augmentation of choice is likely to continue as Credit Accumulation and Transfer Schemes (CATS) and opportunities for study through the European Community Action Scheme for the Mobility of University Students (ERASMUS) and student exchange programmes become more widespread. In all these cases, the contract provides an ideal basis for defining and clarifying content and establishing assessment procedures. Again, there is a parallel with the advantages described with regard to Independent Study but in this particular case the external client is the other degree or other institution.

Finally, learning contracts could beneficially be more carefully integrated into a student's overall educational experience. If contracts were more widely adopted, students would be able, rather in the manner of the Record of Achievement in schools, to build up a developmental profile of their progress through a programme of study. They would be able to take away a Pedagogic Portfolio which could be used as an additional source of reference in regard to their future employment. More importantly, though, such a portfolio could improve the ongoing learning process. The adoption of contracts for all course units would perhaps lead to more thought being devoted by both teachers and students to questions of coherence and progress, to consideration of the respective contributions of different units towards encouraging a wide range of competences, and to explicit attempts to plug gaps in a student's educational experience. Tutors themselves would be able to respond more flexibly to individual student needs. For example, with the spread of schemes to accredit prior experiential learning (APEL), contracts can indicate appropriate starting points and learning programmes for students with very different backgrounds. Students for their part would become more self-aware, more conscious of their own role in the learning process, more actively involved in that process, and more able to fine-tune it to their own very personal needs.

Above all, perhaps the greatest argument in favour of learning contracts is that they can be used to stimulate innovations and experiments in teaching practice and change, incrementally, the broad shape of higher education provision. There is nothing sophisticated, heuristically complex, or pedagogically original about the sort of course unit described in this chapter. The idea is a simple one and has been used by teachers in other institutions. It is described here only in order to broadcast its advantages more widely and *pour encourager les autres*. Simple and unoriginal ideas can have an impact if, following their wider dissemination, enough people are prepared to put them into practice.

'Independent Study' is still in its infancy but has already made a positive contribution to the learning experiences of history students at Manchester Metropolitan University. Students who have participated in Independent Study have encountered new circumstances in which to apply their talents and skills and to develop additional ones. The very favourable comments of the clients, together with the publication and utilisation of a sizeable proportion of the students' work, is itself testimony to how well they have done so. Work placements have, hopefully, enhanced the employability of students.

This type of facilitated learning also appears to meet the particular requirements of certain students who perform better here than in the more conventional areas of their degree programmes. It has certainly offered them a greater variety of experience. Moreover, one of the unexpected but pleasant by-products of 'Independent Study' has been its revelation of student abilities that are not always apparent in a more formal teaching context. In this process, the negotiated contract has proved an excellent basis for establishing a good *rapport* between student and tutor and this should be justification in itself for teachers to contemplate its wider adoption in higher education.

Note

1. A full description of this course unit is available. See D Nicholls, 'Making history students enterprising: independent study at Manchester Polytechnic', in *Studies in Higher Education*, Spring 1992. A fuller version of the present chapter has been published by the Standing Conference on Educational Development, and I am grateful to its editors, David Baume and Sally Brown, for allowing me to reproduce parts of it here.

Chapter Twelve

Learning Contracts and Student Placements with Employers

Wendy Stewart-David

Background

Learning contracts have been used on BA (Hons) Business Studies at Newcastle Business School since October 1990. They are the central feature of a two and a half year management competence development programme, which includes two separate six-month industrial placements and two blocks of college-based work. There are 60 students in each year group. This chapter looks at our experience so far and identifies the benefits gained by students. It also looks at practical difficulties which are yet to be overcome.

When we chose to include learning contracts in the course we hoped that our students would graduate with the ability and motivation to be independent lifelong learners. We hoped to stimulate initiative, creativity and innovative thinking It was also considered important that our students were able to help others learn.

We opted for a scheme in which employers had a vital part to play. At the same time we wanted students to have the opportunity to develop management competences independently of UK-based companies. We felt that if links with specific companies were too tightly imposed, we might destroy the very flexibility and choice we were hoping to offer. We therefore chose to include four separate learning contracts, two based on placement experience and two based on college work of the student's own choice. The structure of the course is shown in Figure 12.1. The shaded areas show the progression from first to final learning contract.

Although it was our intention that work-based experience would lead into the learning contract, we left the individual student to decide how closely the College-based contract should link to a specific company. There were several reasons for this decision. Some students discover that the work chosen for first placement does not suit them and they wish to change direction. We also have a growing number of short-term exchange students from Europe and the USA. The learning contract approach is particularly useful for them, as it

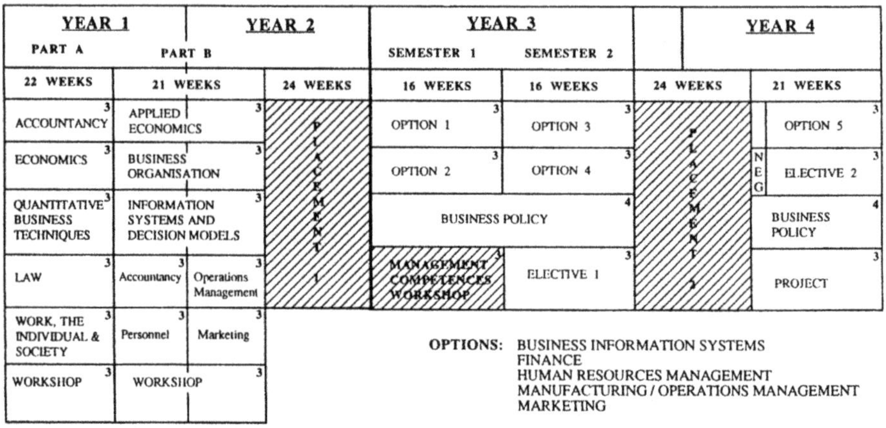

Figure 12.1 *BA Business Studies course structure model*

enables them to devise a learning programme suited to their learning needs and their length of stay. Similarly our full-time overseas students find the learning contract approach helps them relate UK-based studies to the needs of their home environments. A few students develop special areas of interest outside the normal business-based curriculum and the learning contract offers them the opportunity to study an entirely different knowledge-based area or a foreign language, if they so choose.

The work-based learning contracts are assessed by employer appraisal. The college-based learning contracts are assessed alongside all other subjects. This means the assessment strategy has to ensure comparability between students and acceptability to all members of the course team, most of whom use more traditional forms of assessment. We make no claims at present to having found the perfect solution to negotiating assessment. The necessity for consistency and credibility restricts the scope of individual negotiation and this has been discussed by all the parties involved. Students and staff agree that there is a dilemma. Third year work is particularly important in determining the final Honours classification and, naturally, the student is strongly motivated to work towards the best possible classification. Unless the learning contract contributes to this classification, the student will not necessarily give it the same energy as other areas of study, no matter how much the potential for long-term development is appreciated. Our present solution, based on the production of a portfolio with defined assessment

COMPETENCES PROFILE

	Excellent A	Good B	Satisfactory C	Unsatisfactory D
1. WRITTEN COMMUNICATION SKILLS				
Communicates coherently using a variety of business media				
Presents ideas concisely using IT skills and statistical data where appropriate				
Uses appropriate language and style				
2. ORAL COMMUNICATION SKILLS				
Expresses ideas well and presents arguments in a logical fashion in formal business presentations				
Demonstrates, asknowledges and understands non-verbal signals				
Is able to question effectively				
3. ANALYTICAL REASONING SKILLS				
Is able to analyse arguments objectively and to reach logical conclusions based on case study and discussion				
Is able to present well researched and persuasive arguments				
Is able to research and analyse information using a systematic approach - eg, questionnaires and/ or structured interview				
4. GROUP INTERACTION SKILLS				
Shows skill in directing group activities				
Listens actively to others				
Involves all group members, shares information, and supports the ideas of others				

Figure 12.2 *Competences profile* (continues overleaf)

5. **PLANNING AND ORGANISING SKILLS**

Is able to set realistic targets and decide priorities				
Makes good use of time				
Evaluates alternatives and makes appropriate decisions				

6. **PERSONAL STRENGTHS**

Understands own strengths and weaknesses				
Is able to cope with pressure and control emotions				

Figure 12.2 *Competences profile* (continued)

criteria, is described below. It is cautious and subject to further negotiation, but staff and students accept it as reasonable way forward for the time being.

The learning contract programme

Preparation stage

All students beginning the first placement assess their level of competence on the profile shown in Figure 12.2. They have addressed these areas of development in the first year of the course and obtained feedback from tutors and peers. The employer can use the profile to help plan the placement and to evaluate outcomes. We do not ask for a formal learning contract at this stage, though many of the students and employers agree on a contract, even if they do not use the terminology. It is not formally assessed, except as part of the overall placement performance.

The third year college-based learning contract

Discussion stage

The formally assessed learning contract is introduced as soon as the student returns to college from the first placement. We have found that this first few weeks of the third year are crucial to the success of contract learning. It can be a time of uncertainty and anxiety for all concerned and several sessions are devoted to explaining and discussing the rationale of the new approach. Many students expect college work to be quite different from work-based experience. Expectations need to be clarified and often adjusted. The situation at this stage is summed up in the following extract from a student portfolio submitted in January 1992:

My initial reaction was one of reticence and hostility. I thought to myself that this was going to be an attempt to employ 'modern' but previously untested approaches to learning and developing oneself. It was us who were going to be the guinea pigs. Having researched further the learning contract approach, I was glad and also relieved to discover that my reaction is a common one. Research by the Industrial Society shows that the most important criteria for success are first to accept the challenge and second to keep an open mind. M Barrett, year 3 student BA [Hons] Business Studies

The Education for Capability Manifesto is particularly useful at this stage. This makes explicit that the challenge is to staff, students, employers and course designers, and that all parties concerned are collaborating from a sense of common purpose. Students begin to appreciate that we are talking about a joint vision, not about experiments with guinea-pigs. Students also need a clear understanding of the educational principles underlying the approach. We ensure that everyone is aware of the learning cycle of action, reflection, feedback, conclusions and forward planning (Kolb, 1985). Familiarity with the cycle is necessary for effective learning in the management competences contract. It is also necessary to ensure adequate documentation for the portfolio.

We also use the learning styles questionnaire by Honey and Mumford (1982), as this helps students become aware of different learning preferences and encourages them to develop balanced learning habits. The students are asked to read round the subject of development and to propose a reading programme as part of the contract. The reading seems to be helpful in clarifying objectives as well as in the reflection stage.

Starting the learning contract

The final appraisal of the second year placement employer can be a starting point for identifying learning needs and some students find this useful. We have found that other students feel disadvantaged because the appraisal has not been perceived as either useful or developmental. For example, last October some students returned from placements where a number of psychometric tests had been given for development diagnosis. They had already formulated action plans with the help of employers. Others had been appraised by line managers in smaller companies where appraisal was conducted as a form-filling exercise. Some very competent students had a complete profile of A grades and this gave them no advice about next steps. We cannot therefore use employer appraisal as the main method of identifying learning needs. We ask students to identify their needs from as wide a variety of evidence as possible. This will include a review of critical incidents, published management development questionnaires, peer group feedback and advice from academic tutors. At the beginning of the programme students still look to an authority figure as the only legitimate source of feedback and one of the tutor's responsibilities is to help students realise other sources of feedback. One student was quite surprised to discover that her father was considered a valuable source. Although he was a university lecturer, she had not included him in her documentation as a potential mentor! Several other students have parents in business.

After the diagnosis of learning needs, most students say that setting objectives and planning activities present a challenge rather than a difficulty. Many of them have understood the scope of the method by this stage and they start to use the tutor for extra advice. Negotiation about the plan goes ahead without too many difficulties for the student. However, this stage presents the tutor with particular problems. Thirty students sharing one tutor are eager to make a start and the tutor needs to see each in turn. The timetable allowance for this is presently four hours per week, so there is considerable pressure on the tutor who has many other classes and administrative work. This is a major practical problem which threatens the future success of the approach on large undergraduate courses. The quality of the mentoring and the negotiation is arguably at risk even where the tutor is giving considerable extra time to the students.

Assessment requirements

We specify broad criteria which must be recorded in the portfolio and the criteria are derived from the phases of the learning cycle. They include:

a) an account of the process of identifying the learning need;
b) a diagnosis of the student's learning styles and proposals to develop balanced learning habits;
c) a statement of objectives of the learning contract;
d) a plan of action, which will include names of people who will support the contract;
e) identification of witnesses who would be willing to provide the students with written feedback for the portfolio;
f) reflection on the outcomes, including reasons for success and failure;
g) conclusions and action plans for future development.

Given this uniform set of criteria, we are able to derive a mark which can be taken alongside more traditionally delivered subjects. The matter of assessment has been debated by the Business School Executive, by the course team and by the students concerned. We are agreed that scope for individual negotiation in assessment is limited and that we have only a partial answer at present. The approach is undeniably pragmatic because we wish to offer students the chance to count the learning contract to the Honours classification and so emphasise that the learning contract is seen by Newcastle Business School as equal to all other subjects.

Examples of learning contracts

These are recorded on video and they serve as a useful record for future students. The student videos are especially helpful in the early weeks of third year. Activity so far divides into the following categories:

a) contracts using the former placement employer as the mentor and assessor of the activity;
b) contracts using new employers for interviews or visits;
c) contracts involving organising events such as course visits, exhibitions, surveys;
d) contracts designed by, and for, short-term exchange students, often involving visiting local firms;
e) contracts designed by, and for, full-time overseas students;
f) contracts involving joining another course to study a new subject, often a foreign language. These contracts are usually taken by fourth year students instead of a business-based elective;
g) contracts attempted on second placement, all of which are negotiated between the student and the employer.

Conclusions

Student reaction so far has been largely positive once past the early stages. Typical reactions have been that the learning contract has given a much welcome opportunity to do something different, something of particular interest to the individual. Others report benefits which cannot be easily measured. Increase in self-confidence is frequently mentioned, so is enhanced motivation and greater self-knowledge. The scope for networking with employers and improving public relations has been identified as a benefit. Many students have identified a second placement whilst talking to employers about learning contract activities. Exchange students have enjoyed the approach. They particularly like taking the video recording back to their home tutors. Our overseas students won a £250 prize from the senior management for their exhibition learning contract in 1991.

Employers have described the approach as sensible, easily understandable to companies and a promising way of encouraging students to be more flexible. One firm pointed out that future business success depended upon vision, flexibility and capacity for innovative thinking. The learning contract approach encouraged students to 'come out of their functional specialism boxes' and propose new ideas.

The picture, from the viewpoint of the academic, is a mixed one and this is where we need to direct some attention if the learning contract approach is to be successful. The problems of assessment are by now well known, though not insurmountable, assuming a little pragmatism from all concerned.

Motivation of the tutors has not, so far, received much attention and there appears to be an assumption that tutor satisfaction lies solely in seeing students develop. This presupposes numbers of self-sacrificing people who in reality may not exist. At certain stages in the learning contract process the academic tutor will be working excessively long hours interviewing individual undergraduates and this will be on top of the ordinary timetable. In addition, the early stages of the work are difficult because of the anxiety and hostility often experienced by students. This is not a job for the faint-hearted or the half-committed. Time to do research will often not be available and this may well prevent the academic from progressing in conventional career terms.

Two possibilities have occurred to me so far. The first is that we move towards appointing a person, preferably a management development specialist, who will spend much of his or her time facilitating contract learning and who would receive appropriate time reward and recognition for the task. A second possibility is that all engaged in this type of work within academic institutions make sure that it is seen as mainstream academic research.

References

Kolb, D (1985) *Experiential Learning: experience as the source of learning and development*, New Jersey: Prentice Hall.

Honey, P and Mumford, A (1982) *The Manual of Learning Styles*, Peter Honey, UK.

Chapter Thirteen

Negotiating Learning Contracts for Fieldwork Placements in Physiotherapy

Jean Hay-Smith

Students on the four year BSc(Hons) Physiotherapy Degree at the University of East London (UEL) undergo periods of clinical practice as part of their degree course. Each of the four years is divided into three terms of 12 weeks each and in years two, three and four of the course students undertake a total of 10 four-full-time weeks of clinical practice. These periods of clinical practice are interspersed with full-time college attendance. Clinical practice is supervised by a senior physiotherapy clinician on a one-to-one or two-to-one basis and the student is also visited twice by a UEL tutor during the course of the placement.

Availability of enterprise funding enabled us to look at the use of learning contracts in clinical practice. This initiative was begun by Mrs Susan Neville (Principal Lecturer and Clinical Education Tutor) in an effort to encourage student participation in, and responsibility for, their learning. Wolf (1980) has identified this as an important aspect of practice placements.

We selected one cohort of students (45 second year students) to take part in the initiative. In the eight weeks prior to their first clinical placement these students attended a module called 'Introduction to Clinical Practice' and on this module the students looked at the process of setting and negotiating learning objectives. These learning objectives were to be negotiated with the senior clinician in the first week of the clinical placement and covered three key areas of clinical practice, namely:

a) problem-solving (assessment, evaluation, clinical decision-making);
b) treatment management (application of treatment skills);
c) communication.

The objectives were recorded on a form which had been derived from those used by McMaster and Toronto Universities, Canada. Learning resources, methods of assessment and criteria for assessment were also negotiated and recorded and together with the objectives, formed the learning contract. Whilst on clinical placement, students were encouraged to use two learning strategies (work diaries and peer group reflection) as an aid to thinking about their learning and the learning process.

We have just completed the process with the first clinical placement and at the end of the placement evaluation questionnaires were sent to students, clinicians and UEL staff. Further evaluation was possible at the clinical seminars attended by students on their return to the university and a group of UEL tutors reviewed all the learning objectives.

A number of difficulties were encountered by students and staff. First, many students had difficulty differentiating between problem-solving and treatment-management objectives. Second, students found the recording of learning resources and methods of assessment repetitive. Third, the most difficult of all the tasks was setting the assessment criteria. We addressed all these issues in the clinical seminars following the clinical placement and students were asked to identify, and record, potential learning objectives for their next placement.

The majority of students found the writing of work diaries repetitive. We felt this was probably because they tended to write descriptively rather than use them as a tool for reflection. Students were encouraged to continue using this strategy on their next placement but with weekly, rather than daily recordings. Peer reflection was the preferred activity and a further option (a checklist incorporating self- and peer-reflection activities) will be available on the next clinical placement.

Our experience of this placement is that students vary in their willingness to be involved in the negotiation of objectives and the whole learning process. Consequently, included on the assessment form for the next clinical placement was a question for students and clinicians about the extent to which the student was involved in the process.

We are pleased that the response from students, clinicians and staff to the initiative has been largely positive and look forward to evaluating the changes that we have made for the next clinical placement. Students were asked to submit a short assignment entitled 'Discuss the extent to which you felt you have achieved your learning objectives'. Some of the scripts were very good, all were enlightening and at least one student appears to be on the right track:

> Made you realise that clinicals are part of a *learning process*. Prior to lectures, I felt that I would just be expected to work and my emphasis would have been on getting through a patient load, rather than taking my time and instead placing the emphasis on *learning*. Year 2 student, 1991.

References

McMaster University, Ontario, Canada, P Solomon (personal communication).

University of Toronto, Ontario, Canada, R K Ladyshewsky (personal communication).

Wolf, J F (1980) 'Experiential learning in professional education: concepts and tools', *New Directions of Experiential Learning*, **8**, pp. 17–26.

Chapter Fourteen

Learning Contracts for the Industrial Experience of Hospitality Management Students

Isabell Hodgson

Introduction

Learning contracts were integrated into the Industrial Experience programme for Hospitality Management students at Leeds Metropolitan University in 1990. The primary aim was to ensure quality training for all students, thereby reducing the possibility that some students received excellent training while others gained very little.

It was recognised that students placed within the large national companies followed a comprehensive structured programme, often the company's management training programme. However, others who were placed with smaller often independent organisations were treated as 'hands on deck' employees and seldom experienced more than two departments throughout their 48 weeks training.

The learning contract

The learning contract is seen as a framework for structuring and planning the students' learning experience during the industrial component of their course in order to enhance the experience both for the student and the company or organisation.

The student is expected to negotiate the learning contract directly with the industrial supervisor. Both parties have to consider their needs and requirements and the student must have prepared a draft contract prior to the initial meeting. The process of negotiating the learning contract is part of the learning experience and the ability to negotiate, by both parties, will influence the eventual outcome. The objective is not to produce a 'perfect document' but to negotiate and mutually agree the Industrial Experience programme, highlighting potential learning opportunities, consistent with the needs and requirements of both parties. The contract is not 'set in stone' and should encompass flexibility and be open to renegotiation at any stage.

Implementation

After selection of students and employers, several workshop sessions were organised to brief all parties on all the stages, factors and construction of the learning contracts. There were no defined criteria for selection of either students or employers.

Employers from the Industrial Experience working party readily agreed to their involvement in the scheme, as they had all predominantly fulfilled their obligation by providing structured training programmes for students whilst in industry. Other parties, who were known to rely on students initiating their own training, were also approached.

Finally, in July 1991, contracts were agreed and implemented by ten companies from a wide variety of sectors within the hotel and catering industry.

Evaluation and monitoring

Within the first three months of the placement period, all students were visited by one of the tutors who had been involved in the initiating and implementation of the programme. Problems were discussed with all the parties involved and solutions suggested. After six months, students and mentors from industry attended a recall workshop session at the University, when each programme was reviewed.

Summary of employers' and students' observations

Students

1. Learning objectives encompassing the whole year are required for each department, not just for the whole unit.
2. Distinctive approaches need to be adopted for each type of establishment.
3. Learning contracts have enhanced student awareness of methods and systems within the organisation. They have enabled students to evaluate and question more freely.
4. Students who have negotiated contracts are achieving much more from the placement than students who have not.
5. All students agreed they were exerting more effort ensuring they were achieving their objectives and getting as much as possible out of their placement.
6. They all felt the responsibility for learning and achieving was theirs and did not rely on their mentors from industry to supply information and continually motivate them.

7. Contracts have been most successful where both students and mentors have taken a positive approach.
8. Students requested a more structured brief, prior to negotiating with industry (ie, written examples of contracts from previous students).
9. Students suggested that learning contracts should be introduced to other modules within the curriculum to enable students to have gained experience in negotiating skills within college prior to industry.
10. All students found the experience of having to negotiate assessments for their period in industry very difficult, having been accustomed to college tutors setting the criteria for all assessed work.

Employers

1. Where there is a structured programme suggested by a mentor, the student has a blinkered view, accepting that he or she does not need to negotiate any further. Students need encouragement to push for more individual aspects.
2. Where the student has been given a free hand in devising his or her programme for learning, mentors have been fully utilised in assisting with the programme and the student has certainly benefited.
3. In the majority of cases, the contract has encouraged students' awareness of the organisation and the managing of the day-to-day running of the units.
4. Rather than devise a contract within the first week of the training period, employers suggested that students should delay the process until they have completed the induction programme and settled into the organisation. Having achieved this, they were in a stronger position to negotiate, more confidently, a more realistic contract.
5. The contract was assisting students to have a more holistic view of the company.
6. Most students had approached the exercise in a very business-like manner, making it a very worthwhile experience for all parties.
7. Each employer was satisfied that the introduction of learning contracts had been a success with all parties benefiting but was dependent on the motivation and commitment of the individuals involved.

Future proposals

Following the discussions with all parties, it has been decided to withhold integrating learning contracts into all industrial placements until 1993. It was felt that a further study of perhaps 50 students should be evaluated to ensure as many problems as possible could be ironed out prior to launching everyone into the programme. It was also agreed that further training sessions should be planned to ensure all mentors in industry are fully briefed on the expectations and outcomes of learning contracts.

SAMPLE CONTRACT: COMPLETED BY BA 3RD YEAR STUDENT HOSPITALITY MANAGEMENT

Learning Contract
Self-Development

A Review Of My Own Abilities
A review of my own abilities is necessary to assess the contents of the learning contract. The whole point of the learning contract will be dependent on the requirements of the employer, university and myself. The requirements of the employer will become apparent upon primary negotiations with the employer prior to the commencement of the placement. However, I have listed a review of my own abilities and this should help in understanding why my personal requirements from the learning contract may be missing some important areas.

A List of the Review of My Own Abilities
– **Bar Work** – I have a knowledge of bar work. Having worked at various bars, I have an understanding of the service, measures, hygiene, liquor knowledge and some cellar work.
– **Kitchen Work** – I have a sound basic knowledge of food preparation. However, I would like to learn more about food control, wastage, ordering, presentation and menu planning, etc.
– **Restaurant Work** – I have worked in many restaurants so my restaurant skills are more than adequate. I have a high level of confidence with customers and am skilled at silver service. However, I understand that the 'Doves' restaurant at the Resort, Wetherby will have its own service style and methods of service, etc. I would therefore like to learn more about their methods.
– **Reception** – I have never worked behind reception. Although I have been taught at Leeds Metropolitan University how the processes of reception work and have encountered basic reception work, I believe that a real-life situation will be far-removed from the theory.

– **Accounting** – No experience. However, I have studied accounting at the University. I only have a basic knowledge of the work involved.

– **Housekeeping** – I have worked in housekeeping in a Welsh country guest house. However, the methods of cleaning and room presentation were prehistoric and did not follow any standards, routine or hygiene regulations. Having studied Accommodation Management, I would like to put my theoretical knowledge into practice.

– **Banqueting** – I have worked in the banqueting department of the Hilton International, Leeds. I therefore have a sound knowledge of the processes involved. I have helped to plan the layouts, colour schemes etc. of large weddings/parties/conferences.

– The Kitchen –

A List Of Objectives and the Strategies Involved to Achieve These

OBJECTIVE ONE: To understand the menu and ingredients of dishes.
STRATEGY
1. General kitchen experience.
2. Obtain a copy of recipes/ingredients.
3. To gain information as to which dishes/ingredients change due to external conditions eg availability, etc.

OBJECTIVE TWO: To be able to prepare every dish on the menu in the specified time, with the specified resources and to the required standards.
STRATEGY
1. General kitchen appearance.
2. Taking notes of times for cooking, ingredients needed, standards, etc.

OBJECTIVE THREE: To be able to work as a team with the kitchen staff and restaurant staff.
STRATEGY
1. Understand what is required to ensure that everyone's needs are satisfied.
2. Try to create a balance of friendliness with professional attitude.
3. Listen and understand what they have to say.

OBJECTIVE FOUR: To be able to be involved in the control system of the kitchen.
STRATEGY
1. Stock-takes.
2. Ordering.
3. Comparing kitchen output to restaurant sales.
4. Be able to identify where wastage is occurring and offer suggestions as to how, why and when.

OBJECTIVE FIVE: To find out how well the kitchen liaises with the restaurant on ideas such as menu formulation, etc.
STRATEGY
1. General observations.
2. Talk to the Head Chef.
3. Talk to the Restaurant Manager.

OBJECTIVE SIX: To understand the operation of kitchen equipment, maintenance and safety of such machinery.
STRATEGY
1. Listen to Chef's instructions.
2. Read instructions on machinery – look at instruction manuals.
3. Evaluate their efficiency through experience and use.

OBJECTIVE SEVEN: To understand the methods of stock rotation and turnover used in the kitchen.
STRATEGY
1. Listen and utilise instructions.
2. Understand the life of products used – refer to food safety notes and other literature.

OBJECTIVE EIGHT: To understand the different ordering systems for the departments of restaurant, banqueting, etc.

OBJECTIVE NINE: Gain information as to how the change from the Penguin to Resort has brought about change in the kitchen and how the Food Hygiene regulations 1990 have affected the operation of the kitchen.
STRATEGY
1. Talk to the Head Chef.
2. Look at the new policies and the old policies.
3. Look at how the layout, style of service may have changed.

– Reception –
A List of Objectives and Strategies to Achieve these Objectives

OBJECTIVE ONE: To understand generally the tasks and processes involved in reception work.
STRATEGY
1. Experience on reception (both day and night).
2. Achieving the objectives set out (below).

OBJECTIVE TWO: To understand the reservation systems.
STRATEGY
1. Understand and implement the understanding of the processes involved in taking, changing and cancelling reservations.
2. Learn how to take a booking.
3. Learn telephone behaviour.
4. Have a knowledge of the hotel generally, so that any enquiries can be dealt with efficiently.

OBJECTIVE THREE: To be able to quote prices/charges with no trouble.
STRATEGY
1. Learn the rack rates.
2. Identify the seasonal variance in price and demand.
3. Learn banqueting/conference charges in case there are any general enquiries and the appropriate manager cannot be located.

OBJECTIVE FOUR: To have a sound company/hotel knowledge to deal with any general enquiries from customers.
STRATEGY
1. Read company literature.
2. Read hotel literature.
3. Obtain information from general conversation with members of staff.

OBJECTIVE FIVE: To observe Resort Hotel policies as to the way to deal with complaints.
STRATEGY
1. Read company policy.
2. Listen and utilise training on reception.

OBJECTIVE SIX: To learn about other processes involved in reception work.

OBJECTIVE SEVEN: To observe how the policies of reception have changed since Penguin was taken over by Resort.
STRATEGY
1. Compare old policies with new policies.
2. Ask members of staff how the policy change has affected their work.
3. Evaluate the advantages/disadvantages of policy change.

Learning Contract
General Objectives

OBJECTIVE ONE: To achieve everything from the placement that I set out to achieve.
STRATEGY
1. Follow guidelines from departmental objectives (see other sheets).
2. With negotiation between the Resort Hotel and Leeds Metropolitan University.
3. Taking a systematic approach to my training.
4. Realising what resources are available for the collection of data and training.
5. Time plans (as to dates when objectives are achieved).
6. Realising that there are three parties involved in my industrial placement, (the Resort Hotel, Leeds Metropolitan University and myself) and that we all have our own objectives and strategies. In realising this I can ensure that all parties are satisfied.

OBJECTIVE TWO: To be accepted as an effective part of the team.
STRATEGY
1. To try and create a happy and satisfying working atmosphere.
2. To give favours as much as they are taken.
3. To help people out with their jobs and expect them to help me with mine.
4. Share information which would make their job easier.
5. Share tasks in order for them to be performed more quickly and to a high standard.

OBJECTIVE THREE: To create a favourable impression to Resort Hotels in order to achieve respect and the possibility of the Group offering a position after my graduation.

OBJECTIVE FOUR: To observe and understand the changes that have occurred and are likely to occur due to the takeover of the Penguin by Resort.

OBJECTIVE FIVE: To understand and collect information as to how Resort hotels are planning for the future (ie, 1999, demographics, etc).

Other Objectives to be Achieved while at the Resort Hotel, Wetherby

1. To perform an interview for recruitment.
2. To understand the marketing and promotions policies of the hotel and evaluate them.
3. To understand how the hotel markets its facilities towards target markets and how far the hotel utilises customer segmentation.
4. To understand the policies of the hotel and evaluate why these particular policies were formulated.
5. To look at the area of 'CHANGE' ie the Penguin Hotel to the Resort Hotel.
6. To understand, and somehow be involved in, the planning of the facilities and resources of the hotel.
7. Helping to organise generally.
8. An understanding of the difference between head office planning and the hotel's planning.
9. The management structure of the hotel.
10. Maintaining a balance between personality and professionalism.

Chapter Fifteen

Using Student-driven Learning Contracts in Work-based Learning and with Small Businesses

Iain Marshall and Margaret Mill

Introduction

Undergraduates at Napier University in Edinburgh are collaborating with teaching staff and employers in developing learning contracts which earn academic credit towards their degree. The Training, Enterprise and Education Directorate (TEED) are funding the refining of a student-driven model, which can be used in a variety of institutional contexts.

Learning contracts in work-based learning

By encouraging the students to take a large measure of responsibility for

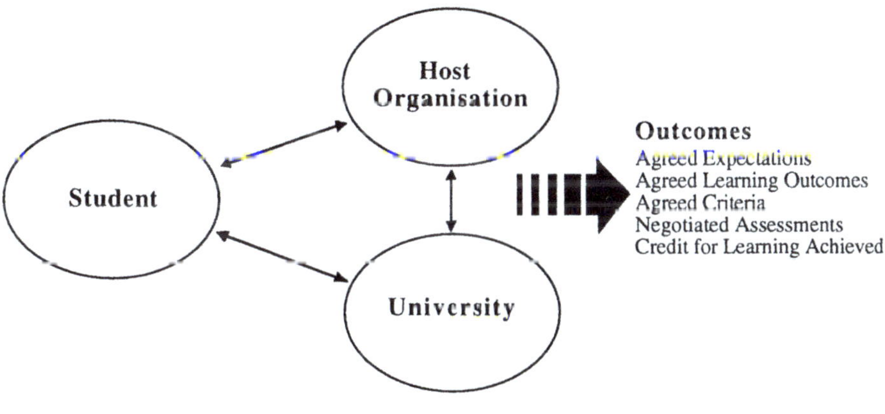

Figure 15.1 *Model of student-driven three-way learning contract*

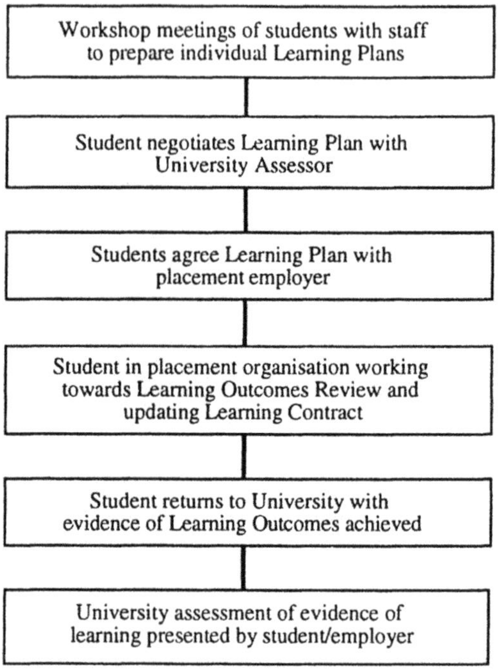

Figure 15.2 *Model of work-based learning process for students*

identifying what they want to learn from the experience of sandwich placements, the motivation of the learner is harnessed to achieving agreed learning outcomes. The model encourages ongoing renegotiation by all three partners. Once they get the hang of it, students are keen to turn learning which they value, into academic credit towards their Honours Degree. Academic staff tend to find the focus on the outcomes of learning somewhat tricky, but the students and the employers can be very helpful! The process in the Napier project looks like the model given in Figure 15.2

Employers of our sandwich students, especially small- and medium-sized companies, greatly appreciate students negotiating what they hope to learn from placement experience, in advance. It saves time and money by avoiding inappropriate matching of student and placement. Students are glad to have the chance to turn relevant learning from experience into real academic credit towards their degree.

Of course, this approach raises a whole range of staff development issues for the University as it shifts the role-relationship between staff and student towards greater learner autonomy. However, a possible bonus to the institution is legitimately to shorten the overall length of a course by offering academic credit for a previously 'dead' period.

There are three good reasons why systems and procedures must be developed which allow students to earn credit from work-based learning which counts towards their degree:

a) in academic institutions, there is a distinct tendency for resources to follow the award of credit;
b) many of our students have an instrumental approach to course work. The award of marks or credit influences the effort they are prepared to put into an assignment; and
c) where employers are participating actively in the process, they express the view that students should be rewarded for achieving relevant learning outcomes.

Assessment of the evidence submitted by the student is central to the award of credible academic credit.

In the learning contract model being developed in Napier University, the following principles and conditions are emerging.

Assessment of work-based learning

Some general principles are that:

a) assessment be collaborative rather than unilateral;
b) assessment be constructive and responsive to learners' needs;
c) the conditions necessary for good assessment must be given a priority in the allocation of time and other resources.

Some necessary conditions are that:

a) there be clear learning outcomes which are agreed between learner and assessor to be relevant to the qualifications sought and valued by the learner;
b) the credit awarded for evidence of learning should fairly reflect the quality of that learning;
c) there be a policy regarding the nature of evidence of learning and a readiness to explore different instruments of assessment;
d) there should be mechanisms which take account of the views of the learner and the employer in arriving at a collaborative assessment;
e) there should be a policy for the professional development of teaching staff and of employer 'mentors' in support of the work-based learner and in the assessment of the evidence of learning which is submitted;
f) there be a structure within an institution where the academic Board of Studies can evaluate its success in achieving its own stated aims and adjust its practices appropriately.

The learning outcome

The fundamental element of the Napier model of work-based learning is the learning outcome. By encouraging the learner to reflect on learning which they already have achieved, or identify learning they will attempt to achieve, attention is paid to specifying learning which is supported by adequate evidence.

Students are encouraged to specify group learning outcomes they plan to achieve from placement, under three headings:

job-related outcomes;
personal development outcomes;
course-related outcomes.

During the planning phase, prior to going on placement, the developing list of learning outcomes is negotiated with staff in the University. A major consideration is that the learning outcomes should be judged to be meeting the aims of the degree. Each student negotiates with a member of the University staff who will be the University assessor of the evidence which the student will offer in support of the agreed learning outcomes. The list of learning outcomes proposed by a student is used as part of the agenda during placement interviews with potential employers. Invariably, further negotiations occur which have to satisfy all three partners – the student, the company mentor and the University assessor.

Throughout the placement experience, the list of learning outcomes is regularly modified and renegotiated between all three partners to the learning contract. Before the student is due to finish the placement, they confirm with the University assessor the list of learning outcomes they wish to be assessed against.

The company mentor receives a print-out of this list in the form of an Assessment Grid, which asks the mentor to confirm whether or not the student, in each case:

a) has indeed accomplished the learning outcome;
b) has provided evidence of understanding against a scale of 1–4;
c) has provided evidence of adding value.

This assessment by the mentor is invariably discussed with the student and sent to the student's University assessor, who has his or her own Assessment Grid (which is asking similar questions of the portfolio of evidence the student submits, in support of their claimed learning outcomes), and arrives at a considered judgement as to the credit to be awarded. By developing professional judgement through experience gained with colleague assessors and students, the question of quality and standards is continually reviewed and refined.

Napier University is moving towards a credit-based system which will incorporate work-based learning but, at present, undergraduates still have to achieve a number of marks from a variety of instruments of assessment which determine their Honours Degree classification.

In developing appropriate systems and procedures at Napier University, it is seen as crucial that the staff who are to operate the scheme are satisfied that they have developed a workable scheme. Where schemes are responsive to needs, then they are liable to vary between one course and another. This will be particularly noticeable in the early stages until examples of 'best practice' emerge.

In the BA/BA (Hons) Hospitality Management, a proportion of third year marks are allocated to work-based learning. This total available mark is broken down as follows:

20 per cent for the quality of the learning plan;
30 per cent for the assessment by the employer;
20 per cent for the portfolio evidence assessed by the University staff assessor;
30 per cent for the viva voce by the University staff assessor.

In the case of the BA(Hons) Business Information Systems, the course team has identified 'core' learning outcomes which the student should attempt to achieve, with additional self-selected learning outcomes submitted by the student. The three categories of learning outcome are retained, and an agreed number of marks are allocated as follows:

30 per cent for evidence of job-related outcomes;
30 per cent for evidence of personal development outcomes;
40 per cent for evidence of course-related outcomes.

It is interesting to note that these schemes attempt to reward evidence of learning, and will discriminate between differing levels of achievement of relevant learning outcomes.

A danger in the move toward a credit-based scheme is that where units of credit are based on units of time (ie, 1 credit = 8 hours of appropriate activity), the discriminatory power of the model is lost. To be regained, it seems to us that we must move on from the simplistic time-based unit of credit toward an acknowledgement of the relevant learning outcomes which can be realistically achieved and demonstrated by a learner. This would allow students to earn more or less credits towards their degree, by way of work-based learning. Where courses are explicit about the learning outcomes, which are at present implicit within the syllabus, the issue of credit transfer, based on credit for learning outcomes achieved, is greatly facilitated.

A significant point which should not be overlooked is that the BA Business Information Management course team have devised an assessment scheme for awarding academic credit and communicated both the procedures and the credit weighting to the students *before* they go on sandwich placement. This clearly has implications for the positive motivation of both University staff and students involved. By comparison, the BA Business Studies staff and students are much less clear, and one consequence of this uncertainty is some evidence of confused and demotivated students on placement. A lesson being learned by the Business Studies staff is that the students benefit from knowing in advance what they have to do to earn academic rewards for providing evidence of learning.

The Management Charter Initiative (MCI) Standards provide Business Studies staff and students with invaluable guidelines as to what might be learned during placement, and it is anticipated that the MCI model will influence the assessment scheme devised by BA Business Studies. The BSc

Civil and Transportation Engineering Course team have, like Business Studies, not grasped the nettle of negotiating and agreeing a scheme with the students before they go on placement. For this BSc course, the equivalent to MCI Standards is the Institution of Civil Engineer requirements for corporate membership.

Staff in both of these courses are, through their involvement in the pilot project, giving their placement students much more support and monitoring than was previously possible. Both course teams continue to meet in workshops with project staff to devise appropriate systems and procedures for the award of academic credit.

Looking to the future, the opportunity to achieve units of CATS credit from work-based learning will begin to blur the distinction between full-time and part-time courses. We can now begin offering people in full-time employment flexible access to higher education qualifications by means of CATS recognition of work-based learning. The learning contract is a powerful mechanism for holding together what has to be learned/demonstrated, how this will be achieved, and how it can be assessed. The conclusion reached by the staff at Napier University is that the award of academic credit for evidence of relevant learning is the engine which drives the process.

The challenge confronting us is to continue to refine appropriate systems and procedures for rewarding evidence of relevant learning. In doing so, we are now addressing the use of work-based learning contracts with employees in small businesses.

Using learning contracts with very small businesses

The process

The entire process of developing a learning contract for training and development and assessing it is similar to our work-based model and is shown in Figure 15.3.

This exciting project at Napier, which targets people in very small businesses, has developed from our work with undergraduates on sandwich placements. The challenge was to find innovative ways of helping busy people to access resources in higher education. People in the small business sector often do not know what *is* available, and could not take the time off work to attend conventional programmes anyway!

Our conception of Open Learning can be thought of as having both a *dissemination orientation*, and a *development orientation*. The former sees knowledge as a valuable *commodity*, existing independently of people, which can be stored and transmitted. The latter sees knowledge as a *process* of engaging with and attributing meaning to the world, leading to an enhancement of personal competence. The evolving model of learner-driven, three-way learning contract which is briefly described, is embedded in a *development orientation*.

The idea of extending the learning experience beyond the classroom and

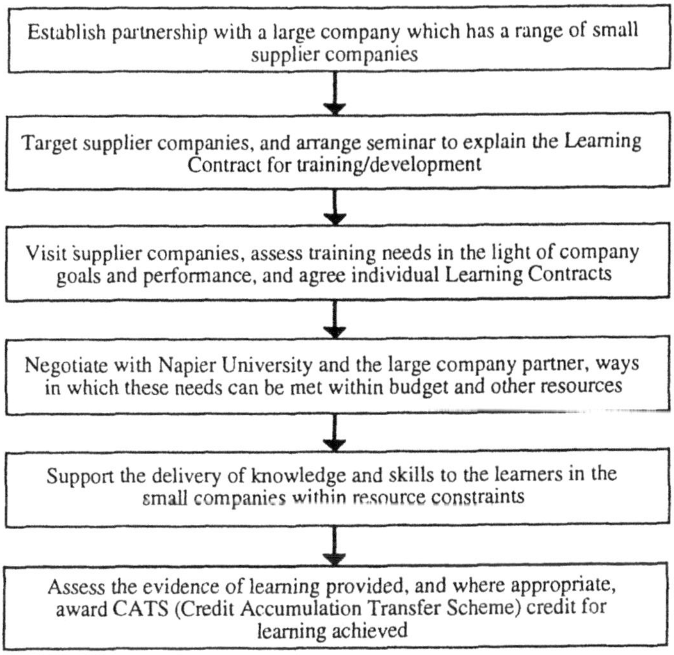

Figure 15.3 *Model of the work-based learning process*

into a work or vocational location is an important part of educational development. In order to accurately target people in small businesses, we established a partnership between Napier University and British Telecom (BT). A large company such as BT, with a philosophy sympathetic to this way of working, allowed us to identify from among their supplier companies a number of companies which could be invited to collaborate in negotiated learning contracts. To begin with, individuals would identify what they wanted to learn in order to improve performance.

The next step is to seek out the appropriate resources from within Napier and BT in order that the learning need is met in ways which are flexible and appropriate to the learner. Having done that, the value to the learner is in improved competence and in the prospect of academic credit towards a qualification.

The learning contract model provides an underpinning structure for this extremely responsive and flexible form of open learning. With the development of Credit Accumulation and Transfer, individuals who produce evidence of achieving agreed learning outcomes can be assessed for the award of academic credit. The benefit to the learner is the targeting of specific needs which are met in ways which are tailored to individual requirements and contribute to improved quality of performance.

SECTION FOUR: USING LEARNING CONTRACTS WITH EMPLOYEES

Introduction

Mike Laycock and John Stephenson

Through the pioneering work of the Learning from Experience Trust (LET) and further support from the Employment Department, the growing recognition of the importance of accrediting work-based learning has led some institutions to seek partnership agreements with companies. By using learning contracts and the Credit Accumulation and Transfer Scheme, employees have been enabled to plan, monitor and review an accreditable programme of learning in higher education institutions that is clearly linked to their own continuing professional development.

Much credit for the early project work must go to Norman Evans, who, when working at the Policy Studies Institute (PSI), conducted research into various aspects of experiential learning and its assessment and, through negotiations with the Training Agency (then the Manpower Services Commission), established the LET. The 'Learning while Earning' (1989) Project (originally entitled 'Making Work Experience Count Towards Graduation for Non-Graduates'), was managed by Gerald Dearden and involved the use of learning contracts with four major employers (including the Training Agency) and four UK universities.

These kinds of 'work-placed' learning contracts make particular demands on higher education institutions and employing organisations to reach agreement on what constitutes *valid* learning, how it can be resourced and managed and what appropriate forms of assessment can be introduced to evaluate the outcomes of such learning. It is in the validation of accreditable learning where employees, academic staff and workplace mentors can, once again, jointly plan, monitor and review learning through the learning contract.

One of the key examples in this section is provided by Clive Robertson whose experience in the area stems from an LET 'Learning while Earning' project originally undertaken with other higher education institutions in 1987/88 and since developed by Oxford Brookes University. The outcomes of the project have recently been published (Employment Department, 1992). Robertson's contribution defines the work-based learning contract, the stages involved in its negotiation and a number of 'recommendations of good practice' including the importance of mutual trust and recognition, the presence of a culture of workplace systems of appraisal, the value of learning sets, the skills and training of workplace mentors, and the identification of learning outcomes and criteria for their assessment.

Anne Brockbank's work at Manchester Metropolitan University also acknowledges the 'Learning while Earning' project in the development of the institution's franchise agreement with B&Q plc whose core is 'the development of competences, achieved through a learning contract mechanism'. Goal-setting is viewed as a crucial activity for success in learning contracts and a number of criteria are identified in order that goals may serve aims. Brockbank also acknowledges the role of company mentors, who are not the participant's line manager and, by virtue of their training and background, have developed the necessary enabling and facilitating skills.

At Roffey Park Institute, the philosophy of self-managed learning informs the whole process of the Master of Business Administration (MBA) programme. Kathy Moore describes a negotiation process whereby course participants agree their learning goals both within their support group (or learning set) and with their organisation. Renegotiation of the contract over time is possible since the organisational settings in which managers work can provide barriers to learning.

For the Certificate in Management (CM) programmes at Bradford and Ilkley Community College, Julie Hinchliffe asserts that the success of the learning contract model depends 'upon the availability and support of the workplace mentor'. The process used to introduce learning contracts included induction sessions for managers and their mentors and workshop sessions for mentors. As other contributors, she points to the importance of staff development for academic staff, mentors and the managers themselves who 'can experience difficulty understanding the approach and getting started on a contract'.

The contribution of Dr Sheila Harri-Augstein and Professor Laurie Thomas offers a novel approach to the writing of what they term 'the Personal Learning Contract (PLC)', a contract which the Self-organised Learner (SOL) negotiates with him or herself as part of a reflexive process of 'learning conversations'. Two parallel 'conversations', task- and learning-focused, are identified. The former reflects on well-practised skills and tasks and the latter is concerned to 'challenge and improve how the learning is carried out'. Using this approach, they identify work undertaken with staff of the Post Office using task- and learning-focused PLCs and discuss its implications for the learning organisations of the future.

Donald Currie, by contrast, reports on an institutional contract, a 'Partnership Agreement' between the Southampton Institute and Southern Water

Services Ltd in which the company sponsors a Fellowship in the Institute's Management Centre. The Fellow is responsible for a range of development including award-bearing courses, research, consultancy and training and development. Tripartite learning contracts have emanated from this main contract for use within the courses and in training and development.

An institutional system for approving individual learning agreements is the subject of the final contribution by Christopher Harris. Anglia Polytechnic University has constructed a central Approvals Board in order to process and validate learning agreements that are outside undergraduate or postgraduate course schemes but which facilitate learning by full-time employees in the workplace and can be accredited within the institution's CATS system. The approval process recognises an 'Enabling learning agreement' which provides the framework within which individual agreements can be ratified. The process obviates the necessity to approve each individual learning agreement. He describes the process in detail by reference to an enabling learning agreement with a group of professionals employed by the local authority.

References

Learning from Experience Trust (1989) *Learning while Earning: Learning contracts for employees*, HMSO, London.

Oxford Polytechnic (1992) *Work-based Learning Contracts*, Sheffield: Employment Department Group.

Chapter Sixteen

Work-Based Learning Contracts

Clive Robertson

Introduction

The project arose from development work undertaken in 1987/88 on work-based learning contracts which is reported by Gerald Dearden in the Learning from Experience Trust publication, *Learning while Earning*. In this early work, the viability of learning contracts as a method of enabling and assessing work-based learning was tested. Four universities, Coventry, Oxford Brookes, Sheffield Hallam and Wolverhampton each worked with a partner company or organisation, Jaguar Cars, Wimpy International, the Manpower Services Commission (later the Training Agency) head office at Moorfoot, Sheffield, and JBS Computer Services, Wednesbury, respectively.

The success of this work and the potential which learning contracts offered for the development of work-based learning prompted the Training Agency, now the Training, Enterprise and Education Directorate (TEED) of the Employment Department, to invite the participating universities to undertake further projects to develop and encourage wider participation in learning contracts. This widening of participation was to be achieved both by involving more companies or organisations and also by involving more academics from a range of disciplines in the universities.

At Oxford Brookes University the following companies or organisations took part in a project which was carried out over two years, from October 1989 to October 1991:

Heathrow Airport Ltd;
Hotel Catering and Institutional Management Association (HCIMA);
National Health Service, Hotel Services Training Unit;
Oxfam;
Oxfordshire Health Authority;
W H Smith Group;
Unipart Group of Companies.

These partners were not only chosen because of their existing links with Oxford Brookes University, but also because of the range of organisational characteristics and working areas which they provided in which to test learning contracts.

A work-based learning contract

A learning contract focuses upon the development and learning needs and intentions of an individual. Work-based learning contracts seek to harness the learning and personal development potential of the workplace and thus provide benefits to the employer as well as to the employee. A work-based learning contract identifies the learning and personal development which an individual hopes to achieve in a given period of time and which can be supported by his or her employer. It describes the way in which this learning and development will be demonstrated and thus can be assessed. Assessment enables the award of academic credit for what has been achieved. The levels at which credit could be awarded and the grading system used in this project were based on the CNAA Credit Accumulation and Transfer Scheme.

The following stages were involved in the negotiation of a work-based learning contract:

a) diagnosis of the *Needs* of the individual and the employer;
b) identification of *Objectives* described as *Learning Outcomes;*
c) identification of *Resources,* those provided by the company and those provided by the Universitity;
d) agreement of a *Timetable;*
e) agreement of the *Evidence of Achievement of Learning Outcomes* which will be available;
f) agreement of the *Method of Assessment* and *Criteria* to be used.

It was an important characteristic of this approach to learning that the contract was agreed between an employee, the employer (normally represented by the line manager) and an academic, and that it would be renegotiated as work progressed or as circumstances changed. Employee and employer were both signatories.

Employers were encouraged to provide support for contractees, perhaps in terms of time allocated for reflection, reading and preparation of evidence of achievement, perhaps by encouraging 'self-help groups' or learning sets to be established or perhaps through mentorial support. The involvement of the line manager in negotiation of contracts was encouraged to ensure their recognition and understanding of the contractee's need for help and support.

An underlying principle of the project was that learning contracts should encourage demonstration of learning achieved through an individual's real work rather than through contrived or specially designed assignments, and thus enable assessment of this work-based learning.

Outcomes

In this project, work-based learning contracts have enabled 32 individuals from different walks of life, from different companies and organisations, with different jobs and different educational backgrounds, to demonstrate learning outcomes achieved at quite different places of work, which have been assessed by academics and described in terms of academic credits.

Some 24 staff at Oxford Brookes University have gained experience of work-based learning and of learning contracts, most for the first time. In the majority of cases, any uncertainty or doubts about the workplace as a source of learning or about its accessibility for assessment, have been replaced by enthusiasm, confidence and a desire for more involvement in this area.

Four external examiners from different institutions, and new to this approach to work-based learning, have, themselves, learned from their involvement in the assessment phase of the project and endorsed the achievements of the participants.

Staff in the personnel and training departments of companies, line managers, colleagues of contractees and workplace mentors have been part of a genuine partnership between higher education and the workplace which has exciting potential for future development.

This potential will only be fulfilled, however, if the lessons learned in the last two years are framed as recommendations of good practice for those who wish to develop work-based learning contracts in the future. These recommendations are as follows:-

a) Work-based learning contracts must be founded upon mutual trust and recognition between academics and those in industry, commerce or the professions. There must be a genuine partnership based on the recognition of mutual benefit, sharing of standards and processes, and a learner-centred approach.
b) Partnerships to be based on mutual trust and recognition require a significant investment of time, energy, enthusiasm, information and goodwill in their development, from all concerned.
c) In the workplace, systems of appraisal which are linked to clearly stated performance or development objectives and a culture which recognises the individual and supports his or her development needs, readily suit the learning contract approach.
d) Clearly stated job descriptions and performance criteria can be readily translated into learning objectives which are made explicit through learning contracts.
e) Individuals engaged in learning contracts should be encouraged to form learning sets or self-help groups within the company or organisation. This may require the allowance of time for meetings and allocation of resources.
f) Those engaged in work-based learning contracts require the support, encouragement, coaching and good counsel of workplace mentors, individuals who have received appropriate training and whose function should be perceived by all as having high status.
g) Learning contracts must clearly identify the outcomes which are expected, the way in which they are to be demonstrated and thus

assessed, and the criteria to be used in assessment. These details need to evolve and to be negotiated and so the first draft of the contract should offer broad indications of directions, goals and assessment methods to enable the contractee to get started. As he or she takes ownership of learning and develops a working relationship with a workplace mentor and/or academic tutor, so details can be agreed and included in the learning contract.

h) Contractees need to know the level and quantity of academic credit which they might aim towards, but these are targets which must be seen as such and must evolve from formative assessment of learning achievements as the contract progresses or from formal Assessment of Prior Learning (APL). Targets are likely to change as circumstances at work or in domestic life alter, or with a contractee's pace of learning and development.

i) Work-based learning contracts may require the support of academics who can act as tutors. The academic can help to identify learning outcomes which can be achieved at the workplace, advise on study skills and approaches to learning, encourage reflection and evaluation, and encourage contractees to extend their perspectives beyond the systems, methods and manuals of the company or organisation. An academic tutor can support a number of learning contracts by advising a learning set or self-help group within a company.

j) For work-based learning contracts to be cost-effective, the workplace mentor should, for the most part, provide the support and advice on study skills and approaches to learning, described above. The skills acquired by individuals in becoming mentors should themselves attract academic credit. Academic tutors might need to become routinely involved in learning contracts when higher-level academic credit is the target, although even in these circumstances only occasional and focused input may be required.

k) Through the use of clearly defined objectives expressed as learning outcomes, assessment methods and criteria, workplace assessment becomes possible. Individuals who have undertaken appropriate staff development can act as workplace assessors and their assessment can inform, complement or replace the assessment by academics. It is essential, however, that individuals who are external to the company are involved in quality assurance and assessment moderation and these should, in the short to medium term at least, be academics from institutions of higher education or individuals with previous external examining experience. Appropriate quality assurance procedures are necessary if the credibility and validity of work-based learning through learning contracts is to be ensured.

l) It is essential that, whatever support system is developed within a company or organisation (including or not including academics), the contractee takes ownership of learning and development goals and is pro-active in using resources made available to support him or her.

m) If the learning outcomes are to be expressed in terms of academic credit to enable contractees to take advantage of Credit Accumulation and Transfer Schemes, then it will be necessary for the credit rating to be verified through the quality assurance procedures of an institution of higher education. This will ensure recognition of credit and transferability of credit between the workplace and institutions of higher education.

Reference

Learning from Experience Trust (1989) *Learning while Earning: Learning contracts for employees*, London: HMSO.

Chapter Seventeen

Learning Contracts and a Company Franchised Programme

Anne Brockbank

The ancient Greeks prioritised 'thinker' over 'crafter' and Western educationalists have perpetuated the division between academia and working practice. The great divide between craft and scholarship continued in Britain until the Robbins Committee (1963) launched a reconsideration of higher education. The Robbins principle recommended higher education for all who are qualified to profit by it and who wish to do so. In addition, Robbins emphasised the application of knowledge to the world of everyday life and work.

The Learning while Earning Project (Learning from Experience Trust, 1989) aimed to create a significant link between the world of formal education and the world of work, using learning contracts as the assessment vehicle. A learning contract is: 'an individually negotiated learning agreement between an employee, the employer, and an academic' (p. 3) and involves:

a) new learning on the part of the participant;
b) learning that is academically assessable;
c) learning that benefits the employer as well as the employee.

The classic learning contract proceeds in four stages:

a) learning intentions of the participant;
b) learning activities to be undertaken by the participant;
c) mode of presentation of the evidence that learning has been achieved;
d) the methods of assessment to be used.

Participants in programmes using learning contracts have reported increased confidence and enhanced performance and, some, who saw themselves as non-starters in higher education, have found themselves on the way towards a diploma or degree.

Early experience of learning contracts in four companies showed that participants often need to re-negotiate their contract in terms of time or content. Participants are at the mercy of 'the needs of the business', which may take priority over learners' activities. The interest and support of supervisors/line managers have been identified as crucial for learning contract survival, as well as the line manager's own level of coaching and counselling skills.

The CNAA Certificate in Management (CM) offered by Manchester Metropolitan University is a flexible, post-experience qualification designed for managers at work, and encourages the use of learning contracts as well as other modes of self-managed learning. The University is presently arranging a franchise agreement with B&Q plc to jointly deliver the certificate to the company's assistant managers. The core of the programme is the development of competences, achieved through a learning contract mechanism. Support for participants is to be provided by company mentors who are not in a 'line' relationship with the participant, as there is a wealth of evidence which supports the benefits of such an arrangement.

The starting point for the Certificate in Management is the Management Charter Initiative (MCI) Level 1 range of competences, which forms the basis for the competency profiles, developed by B&Q, for managers at all grades in the company. Company competences are linked to performance criteria in the form of behavioural outcomes or goals – perfect material for learning contracts. An example of one competence category appears in Figure 16.1.

	NEGOTIATING : Range of performance criteria
a)	Provides support to others while negotiating by preparing a factual case and sticking to this brief.
b)	Negotiates successful technical outcomes by comparing options to prove case and backing this up with in-depth technical knowledge.
c)	Achieves business targets by bargaining assertively with internal and external suppliers whilst maintaining sound working relationships.
d)	Obtains optimum benefit to the company when negotiating by using initiative, and trading-off to reach a mutually satisfactory agreement.

Figure 16.1 *A Competence Example: Negotiating*

The company conducts annual appraisals based on 24 competence categories and a manager's competence profile is compared with an ideal profile for each grade. This forms the basis, for participants on the certificate programme, of the Manager's Competence Audit, the first stage in goal-setting for the learning contract.

Goal-setting

Setting goals is a crucial activity for success in learning contracts, mobilising the participant's energy and attention and motivating him or her to search for strategies to accomplish them. Goal-setting proceeds through three stages:

a) Declaration of intent.
b) Clarification of an aim.

c) Setting of goals in terms of objectives (outcomes).

For instance, a participant wishing to develop the *negotiating* competence is likely to begin from a **declaration of intent**:

I need some negotiation skills – that last meeting was a disaster.

When this develops into an aim it might become:

I'm unprepared in negotiation meetings. I can do something about that.

The participant's goal(s) may include:

Before my next negotiation meeting I will prepare a factual brief and stick to it during the meeting.

For goals to serve aims they must fulfil the following criteria and be:

a) **stated as outcomes**. For stating goals in terms of outcomes a useful tool is the 'past-participle approach', eg, 'brief prepared'; 'negotiation achieved'; 'skill acquired, practised, used';
b) **clear and specific**. Making goals clear and specific is not as easy as it sounds, eg, 'being a better negotiator' is not specific, while 'preparing a factual brief for my next meeting' is;
c) **measurable and verifiable**. If the goal is clear and specific then it is verifiable (measurable). Counting is one way of verifying but any defined outcome is capable of being measured, at the very least by its presence or absence;
d) **realistic**. Realistic goals are essential for learning. Nothing deflates the learner more than failure, either due to factors outside his or her control or because the goal was beyond his or her reach. Recognition of the resources necessary for goal-realisation, environmental obstacles, and the limits of personal power will lead to realistic goals;
e) **substantive**. Substantive goals develop from a clear definition of the desired competence or problem situation, and they will address it directly;
f) **in keeping with personal values**. Participants pursuing goals which are in conflict with their belief systems have a struggle with learning. For example, a participant may find the idea of 'lying' in negotiation repugnant and his or her goals might accommodate a 'no lying' clause; and
g) **set in a reasonable time frame**. The time frame for goal-realisation should be established at the setting stage.

For goals to be workable, all seven of these criteria should be in place. Just one missing can make the goal flawed and unworkable for the participant. For this company certificate the role of mentor is crucial in the development of goals which are realistic, substantive, clear and specific, time-defined and measurable against outcomes. Also, mentors will enable participants to explore their own value systems and set goals accordingly. The skills needed for an effective mentoring relationship are complex and elusive for many working managers

The company mentors

The company presently uses personnel and training professionals as mentors, and this makes sense as, by virtue of their training and background, they are likely to have developed the enabling and facilitating skills which characterise the true mentoring relationship. Additional mentors will be found among store managers whose profile indicates the presence of appropriate skills or whose potential for mentor training has been identified in appraisal. The company will offer mentor training to nominated managers. Participants on the certificate programme will be offered a mentor who is not their line manager as research evidence reveals that line managers acting as mentors experience role conflict.(Arnold and Davidson, 1990).

The Certificate programme

At induction day, participants will be enrolled and introduced to the programme (and each other). Mentors, company staff and academic staff will work with participants on their competency profiles which, by comparison with the ideal profile for their grade, enables them to complete the Management Competence Audit. This highlights possible areas for development and the participants will be able to consider their own learning needs in relation to the programme. Shortly after induction, participants will meet privately with their mentor to agree their first learning contract.

Taught inputs are available to participants as and when they require them and learning contract reviews will usually occur within three months of each taught input. Participants present four completed learning contracts in their portfolio at assessment.

References

Arnold, V and Davidson, M (1990) 'Adopt a mentor: the new way ahead for women managers', *Women in Management Reviews & Abstracts*, **5**, 1.

Learning from Experience Trust (1989) *Learning while Earning: Learning contracts for employees*, London: HMSO.

Robbins Lord (Chairman) (1963) *Higher Education*, Report of a Committee of the Privy Council, London: HMSO.

Chapter Eighteen

The Use of Learning Contracts in a Self-managed Learning MBA Programme

Kathy Moore

At Roffey Park Institute, a two-year part-time executive Master of Business Administration (MBA) programme, validated by the University of Sussex, was introduced in January 1990. There are currently three cohorts underway. The cohorts are small with 12–18 delegates on each programme and the average profile of a delegate on the programme is a middle/senior manager age 39 with at least eight years' experience of being a manager. Participants come from all sectors of industry and range from owner/managers to managers in blue chip/multinational organisations. There is also a mix of public and private sectors.

The entire course is based on the principles of learner responsibility and accountability. Participants thus manage their own learning and assessment, individually and collectively. There are six key elements of the programme:

a) the philosophy of Self-managed Learning (SML);
b) mapping the field;
c) the learning set;
d) the assessment process;
e) tutorial and organisational support; and
f) the learning contract (and academic budget).

The philosophy of Self-managed Learning (SML)

The programme is rooted in core values about the process of learning:

a) managing is an active process;
b) managers need to demonstrate that they can manage;
c) managers are required to make sophisticated and difficult judgements and therefore it is appropriate that they should submit their

judgements to the scrutiny of peers as part of the management development process; and

d) managers should manage their own learning if they are also to manage others.

Mapping the field

On the MBA programme the first phase (seven months) is a time for participants to write a learning contract and to see how a range of experts define management. At the end of this phase they have to produce a learning contract and an essay of up to 20,000 words analysing the field of management as they see it.

The learning set

The set provides another accountability framework, and a challenge to critics who see self-managed learning as merely self-indulgent or lacking in rigour. The set consists of a group of five or six managers with a set adviser or two co-set advisers. The set offers support and challenge and the benefit of each individual's experience. For most managers, the experience of working as part of a set tends to be very positive and powerful. Managers value the opportunity to work with others with whom they can be totally honest:

> It was very personally stressful but beneficial – I had one or two intense periods of time that were very painful but I know I was learning. It was done in a way that I found very constructive ... it was done primarily through the sets but also through the set advisers.

Assessment

Assessment takes place at two stages in the programme; Stage 1 at the end of phase 1 and Stage 2 at the end of phase 2.

Stage 1

At the end of phase 1 the two documents produced (the learning contract and the extended essay) are assessed to determine whether the individual has shown the potential to achieve Master's level at the end of phase 2. There are certain assessment criteria set down by the college that work must meet but further assessment criteria are determined by the set. The external examiners are also involved at this stage. Their role is to assess the process by which the sets have worked rather than the content of any individual piece of work.

Stage 2

The learning contract, including the objectives agreed originally and renegotiated over time, provide the basis for a collaborative assessment process at the end of phase 2:

> Anyone managing their own learning should be able to judge their own work ....

However, these self evaluations need to be checked with others, and so the course requires that the individual's peers (the set) form a crucial 'check and balance' on the personal judgement.

Additionally, employers, external examiners and the set adviser are involved in the process which can, therefore, be far more rigorous than traditional methods. Although peer-led, the process can nevertheless result in student failure:

By adding the set adviser's judgement, the useful 'expert view' of a traditional assessment process has an equal voice and the decision on a pass or fail has to be reached by consensus.

Where consensus is impossible, external examiners are more directly involved.

Tutorial support

A key person in the process of tutorial support is the set adviser. Possible roles, which can be the subject of negotiation, include:

a) ordinary set member: giving information and ideas;
b) catalyst: doing something that no one else is doing, such as confronting issues that no one else is prepared to;
c) process consultant: helping with the process by which things are done, such as conflict resolution or effectiveness reviews;
d) link-person: acting as a contact with other interested parties such as employers;
e) adviser: identifying resources and ground rules by which course members have to abide.

Organisational support

Delegates are encouraged to find a mentor in their organisation so that a bridge is maintained into the organisation's needs and direction. An instrument is used to help managers to decide upon the type of relationship they would like from such a mentor in order to assist their choice.

The learning contract

The learning contract is drawn up in phase 1 and provides the programme of study for phase 2. During phase 1 delegates work with their set to determine the content of their contract within the context of personal managerial and organisational style. To assist this process, we encourage delegates to work through the following questions:-

1. Where have I been?
2. Where am I now?
3. Where do I want to get to?
4. How do I get there?

5. How will I know if I have arrived?

Questions 1 and 2 help to clarify learning needs and question 3, defined learning goals. Question 4 gives the plan of action and question 5 provides the basis for assessment.

The learning contract is, however, a two-way process. Managers are expected to agree their learning goals, first with their support group (or set) and second with their organisation. As such, SML represents a very concrete way of tying management development directly into organisational strategy, which would appear to be a growing concern in organisations today. The learning contract is also about getting learners to think about the process of learning itself.

This initial learning contract is not fixed. Participants are able to renegotiate their contracts over time. Evaluation research does show, however, that perceptions of negotiation can vary considerably and can be seen by some participants as an 'admission of failure' or a 'miscalculation'. The 'blank slate' approach can also be heavily criticised on valid managerial grounds. Thus, one participant pointed out that, far from operating with a 'blank piece of paper', managers invariably face barriers to learning because of their organisational settings. Such barriers should be acknowledged in the initial contract, thereby reflecting the realities of organisational life.

The academic budget

The academic budget is a sum of money set aside for each individual to fund tuition in phase 2 of the MBA in order that they successfully complete their learning contract. Money allocated from the budget must relate to specific identifiable items in an individual's learning contract and must be approved by the individual's learning set. The academic budget gives individuals the flexibility to carry out their learning contract in the most appropriate way to meet their own particular learning objectives.

Examples of learning contract elements

The following give examples of elements from MBA learning contracts.

How am I going to get there and how will I know If I have arrived?

How am I going to get there?

Task: Increased background knowledge and understanding of:

- Strategic Management;
- Marketing;
- Finance and Accounting;
- Human Resource Management.

Method:
Reading.
Residentials/Set meetings/Workshops/Seminars/ Tutorials, where appropriate.
Practical experience, where appropriate.

How will I know if I have arrived?

Output: Written paper with illustrations of practical experience as appropriate.
Verbal report to the set on feedback received from mentor.

Aim

Become and establish myself as manager of an independent business unit or profit centre in an IT-based function with a budget of more than £1.5 million and/or more than 15 personnel. Depending on the company size and structure, this would be a director position.

In general, the deliveries will be phased throughout the course, especially the Human Resource items. They usually require initial actions, which need to be discussed in the set, some time for practice and then a final review in the set.

General

Objective: Increase general knowledge and skills in the field of management to be able to fulfil my job more efficiently and satisfactorily.
Method: Participating at residentials, sessions and set meetings.
Criteria: If relevant for me or my position, providing oral or written feedback to the set about my evaluation and experience with the subjects/issues as well as resulting actions and plans.

Dissertation

Objective: Learn about management of change including aspects from systems theory, evolutionary development, paradigm shifts, chaos theory, organisational and human behaviour, implementation strategies, etc. From my point of view, this is essential for management in future in order to survive or thrive in business.
Method: Study, reading and practical implementation.
Criteria: Demonstrate knowledge, reflect experience and skills by issuing an essay and a 30-minute presentation covering the aspects above at the end of the course.

Human resources and people skills

Increase TA 'adult' level and increase level of understanding and acceptance of people who perform below my level of expectation. I think this well help to perform more efficiently in business.

Study TA material and suggestions and implement in practice.

Issuing a paper summarising my strategy and experiences of putting this into practice as well as requesting feedback from Set.

Human resources and people skills

Get overview of evaluation, appraisal and assessment strategies, methods, techniques and key measures in order to give a better and more helpful feedback concerning performance at work, improve selection, promotion and career development methods.

Reading and practical experience.

Demonstrate understanding by issuing summary of main aspects, experiences and implementation strategies, if appropriate.

Operations management

Objectives:Learn about recent research findings and trends in service management.
Method: Reading and practical work.
Criteria: Issuing a paper summarising key points and, if appropriate, my strategy and experiences of putting this into practice.

Strategic management

Working for a company that is undergoing major changes, not always being in control of the timing, brings strategic management sharply into focus. It will require large adjustments by everyone to accommodate radical change and it is evident that not all will be able to adjust. While being familiar with some of the aspects of this subject from my work as a general management consultant, a more formal study of the field is sought. It will be interesting to compare the theory and practice in a company that is undertaking a major reorganisation.

Strategic management

A paper on strategic management. The paper will:

a) map the basic concepts;
b) use relevant models, where considered appropriate;
c) indicate how the subject generally relates to the management of change;
d) use research and other findings based upon reading, the workshops arranged during phase 2, my past and current experience, discussions within my organisation, discussions within other organisations if possible, and discussions within the set.

Each of the above papers will also include a formal presentation to the set of about 30–45 minutes duration.

Chapter Nineteen

The Use of Learning Contracts for Work-based Management Education and Development

Julie Hinchliffe

During 1990, prior to the design of the CNAA Certificate in Management (CM) and the redesign of the CNAA Diploma in Management Studies (DMS) programme at Bradford and Ilkley Community College (BICC), in-depth research was conducted within the Bradford district to investigate the views of employers and managers on management education and training.

The most significant finding was that the vast majority of employers and managers advocated a stronger link between the learning and development on management education programmes and the manager's workplace. Consequently, the design team had discussed how this issue could be addressed and had concluded that the learning contract could be a useful mechanism for enabling managers to undertake work which, whilst still meeting the requirements of a national academic award, would be of relevance and value to themselves and to their employing organisation. Other advantages, the team believed, would include greater emphasis upon self-direction and choice; a student-centred approach which would place more responsibility on managers for their own learning and development; and an opportunity for more effective collaboration with the workplace.

The learning contract model developed drew upon the work of Boak and Stephenson (1987). It was recognised that the success of the approach would depend, to a great extent, upon the availability and support of a workplace mentor. On the CM programme, the provision of a workplace mentor was stipulated as a compulsory requirement (in accordance with CNAA guidelines).

BICC entry requirements for the DMS programme indicated that the provision of a workplace mentor was highly desirable but not a compulsory requirement for acceptance onto the programme. A College mentor was to be provided for any manager who was unable to obtain a workplace mentor. This decision was underpinned by a recognition that it was not always possible for managers to obtain mentorship support from the workplace. It was felt that DMS applicants who lacked positive employer support should not be denied access to management education. However, whenever possible, it was intended that the contract be a tripartite agreement between the programme member, tutor and workplace mentor. From a cohort of 50 managers on the DMS programme, 49 have obtained workplace mentors.

The process used to introduce the learning contract approach included:

a) induction sessions for managers and their mentors where the potential advantages of the approach were discussed and blank and exemplar contracts were provided as a basis for discussion;
b) a professional development team workshop built into the programme for one hour a week. During this time, programme members were to negotiate learning contracts with the staff team. It was also intended that programme members would form action learning sets which would serve as a catalyst, a sounding-board and a support system for the selection and implementation of learning contracts;
c) the establishment of a personal tutor support system so that the progress of managers could be monitored rigorously and additional support could be provided if required;
d) workshops for mentors throughout the programme, to facilitate discussion, provide guidance and resolve issues as they might arise; and
e) visits to the workplace by members of the staff team.

Valuable feedback had been received from managers and their mentors. The majority of managers on the programme liked the approach because they felt that it enabled them to undertake work which was relevant to their own learning needs. The response from mentors was almost entirely complimentary. However, the introduction of the learning contract approach also created difficulties. The major problems experienced were:

a) The approach, because it focuses more strongly on individual learning needs, is resource-intensive. A larger staff team is required during the professional development team workshop period. Furthermore, one hour per week does not appear to allow sufficient time for negotiation of contracts.
b) The kind of shift in approach does require appropriate staff development. Increasingly, staff are seen as facilitators – not lecturers. There is a need for a more individualised approach to negotiate and agree contracts; increased liaison with mentors and employers; and the need to work more effectively as a member of a

team in, for example, the shared assessment of contracts. All this demands different skills and more time.

c) The need to establish efficient administrative systems also adds to the workload. For example, managers' progress on contracts has to be monitored rigorously and recorded. There has to be a system in place to record the processing of contracts to ensure that contracts are passed (within a reasonable time span) from one tutor to another, and that it is known where in the system contracts handed in for assessment can be located.

d) Some managers can experience difficulty understanding the approach and getting started on a contract. Some (a minority) have commented that it is easier (preferable) to be told what to do rather than negotiate their own learning activities.

There is also the possibility of inadequate (or inappropriate) support from mentors. For example, some mentors may place too much emphasis on workplace activities, perhaps to the detriment of managers achieving the requirements for the award. This raises the question, 'Who are our clients – the individual managers or their mentors/employers?'

These were some of the difficulties experienced in introducing and implementing a learning contract approach. However, despite these difficulties, there is a great deal of enthusiasm for the approach amongst managers, mentors and tutors and the learning contract is often perceived as an extremely useful tool for management development.

Reference

Boak and Stephenson (1987) 'Management learning contracts: from theory to practice', *Journal of European Industrial Training (JEIT)*, **II** 4 and 6.

Chapter Twenty

Learning Conversations and the Personal Learning Contract: A Methodology for Enabling Work-based Learners to Become More Self-organised

Sheila Harri-Augstein and Laurie Thomas

Introduction

Our human resources are our richest asset, but we are not offering the best opportunities for individuals to develop themselves. The climate of uncertainty and escalating change creates new demands, yet education and training are not meeting the requirements of industry and society, nor the needs of the vast majority of individuals. We need people whose vision is that of personal responsibility, personal competence, compassion and creativity. In our experience this can best be achieved by enabling everyone directly to address their own learning.

Varieties of learning contract

There are many views of what a learning contract can be. The primary learning contract, from our experience, is the one which the learner makes with him or herself. We call this the *Personal Learning Contract (PLC)*. Other-organised learners can only contract to submit to being taught or instructed. Self-organised Learners (SOLs) exercise their freedom to learn by committing themselves to self-defined PLCs.

Two stages of awareness

The SOL can be seen to be conducting two parallel 'conversations' – task-focused and learning-focused conversations. The first involves a growing awareness of the doing of the task in hand. Often well-practised tasks and skills stabilise into robot-like routines which become lost to conscious control and we just do them. Car-driving, chairing a meeting, reading, paperwork and even problem-solving are just a few examples of where this takes place. But, to meet higher standards, such 'task-bound robots' need to be challenged and brought back into awareness and flexibly rebuilt. This can be achieved by an engagement in task-focused learning conversations. The second has an extended time span and may encompass a whole series of task-focused conversations. This second stage of awareness is learning-focused. It is concerned to challenge and improve how the learning is carried out.

Self-organised Learning works. Often startling results are achieved in improving job performance and educational achievements, learning skills and creative abilities. In taking on responsibility for their own learning people become more motivated and involved. They also work better in teams. SOLs engage in activities which demonstrate that they are accepting responsibility for their own learning, rather than being dependent on others' initiatives and directives.

SOLs are able to appreciate the dynamic nature of the learning process and to strive continuously for greater self-organisation. They are able to challenge existing, partially developed skills and learn how to learn so that such skills are transformed to achieve greater competence by redefining set tasks, and the skills required to achieve them, in their own terms. This generates new dimensions of personal innovation and experimentation. Striving for a 'quantum-leap' improvement in their *capacity to learn*, which carries over into all subsequent activities, they are better able to learn from experience 'on-the-job', to learn from a training course, from experienced colleagues and from their own or others' successes and mistakes. SOL becomes a way of life, on-the-job, and in all personal and social contexts.

Stages of learning conversations

The first stage of a learning conversation concerns itself directly with how personal meanings, anticipations and actions can be reflected upon and reviewed. Personally negotiated learning contracts enable learners to model their own learning and to generate effective feedback about their performance. By understanding the process, they see learning as a skill which can itself be learnt. They are able to observe, reflect, analyse, search, formulate, review, judge, decide and act on the basis of creative encounters with themselves. For the experienced manager and naive trainee alike, this often proves to be an intellectually challenging and emotionally difficult enterprise. It involves as much feeling as thought. The quality of learning depends on a capacity to develop ourselves into new levels of competence.

The central activity is the negotiation of a series of PLCs but as these develop, sorties into the whole life-conversation become necessary for deeper insights into personal needs or relevances. It is this which maintains motivation within ongoing cycles of PLCs. If a PLC flounders through lack of skill, the conversation is steered to the learning-to-learn level when partially developed skills become challenged and opportunities for developing new skills are explored. Thus, the dynamics of a learning conversation grow out of individual needs and the diagnosis of strengths and weaknesses. SOLs can organise and structure a self-development programme which can be rigorously monitored and reviewed.

Many potential self-organised learners are unable to manage their own learning, not because they do not wish to, but because they do not know how. The PLC is a conversational procedure which supports them. It starts as a simple algorithm for identifying:

a *Topic*;	T
a *Task* in relation to the topic;	T
specific *Purposes* in relation to the task;	P
a *Strategy* for achieving these purposes;	S
the anticipated and actual *Outcome*;	O
criteria for *Reviewing the quality* of the outcome;	R
and *Reviewing this cyclic process* as a whole.	R

Purposes, strategies and outcomes exist as part of a nesting set of intentions, behaviours and results. During this iterative process of experimentation, it becomes possible to reflect upon and identify relevant resources for learning. As these are accessed, the SOL can plan and implement one or more alternative strategies for achieving specific purposes, depending on their familiarity with the resource. The PLC is thus a dynamic conversational vehicle for actualising the process of learning. It is the all-purpose tool for guiding the learning conversation. It focuses on the doing of a task and on awareness of learning.

By planning, carrying out and reviewing their learning in the framework offered by the PLC, individuals can develop their capacity to learn. There are essentially five main steps within the PLC:

a) negotiating a learning activity;
b) carrying this out in an actual situation;
c) self-debriefing of actions taken;
d) reviewing the PLC by retrospective comparison with (a);
e) self-diagnosis of learning strengths and weaknesses, and planning a new cycle of PLC.

These represent the essential activities for enabling the learning to develop. It is this experience that enables learners to monitor and control their learning in personally relevant, significant and viable ways.

Experience of many thousands of PLCs has been enabled by the Centre for the Study of Human Learning (CSHL) in its action research projects. Many thousands more have been supported by CSHL-trained SOL coaches in the Post Office. All we can do here is indicate a few topics.

Task-focused PLC's
To improve my handling of difficult postmen.
Getting the best out of my team in the two hours before dispatch.
To understand the use of paperwork in my section.
To get a better performance out of Bill.
Responding rapidly to my team's needs when the automatic sorter breaks down.
To try out various trouble-shooting tactics 'on the floor'.
To improve my organisation of the first hour of my shift.

Learning-focused PLCs
To reflect upon how I learned to prepare myself for a new duty.
To explore how I can improve my judgement of the work rate of a group.
To investigate how I can better intervene to increase manual sorting productivity.
To develop my 'mind map' of what is going on in related areas.
To explore how I make judgements about my staff.
Using my past experience to understand how I identify the state of traffic in my area.
To explore what's really involved in leading my team.

Results from the Post Office project

Results valued by learners themselves

The primary purpose of Self Organised Learning is for individuals to become more involved in their own learning. Thus the primary perspective on the changes produced by learning conversations is that of the learners themselves. Learners logged the following in their personal learning contracts:

a) I enjoy work and life more. I feel more alive. I actually find myself looking forward to work;
b) I want to learn. I can make sense of my job. I am interested. I find all sorts of questions bubbling up. I can see what I ought to know and what I ought be able to do; and that's half-way to learning it;
c) I learn more easily. I learn quicker, I am interested in the detail because I see the relevance. I find myself setting higher standards – why should there be all those mis-sorts? Why isn't my throughput higher?;
d) I am more questioning. I want to understand why things happen the way they do – does it have to be like that? I surprise myself with the ideas I am having. Some don't work but a lot of them are really quite good and I have improved my (control) area in all sorts of little ways;
e) I actually seek feedback. I find myself judging my own performance and then I want to know whether my boss agreed with me;

f) I think more about what I do. I find myself going over my day in my head on the bus going home. Not only that, but I reflect more about the long term – do I really like what I am doing – what are the prospects of special (assignments) or of swapping duties?;
g) I am really beginning to understand how the office works;
h) I find myself remembering all kinds of things I have not thought about for years. I really do have a lot of skill knowledge and experience that I did not know I had. I am beginning to understand myself a lot better – why I do what I do;
i) I find myself worthy to be part of the team. I fit in more easily. I can co-operate without feeling taken over. I am my own man, but I really want the office to do well.
j) What has really surprised me is the kick I get out of helping other people

Results valued by learners' manager

The learner:

a) is more motivated;
b) appears to get more job satisfaction, higher morale;
c) takes more pride in his work;
d) is easier to work with (not so prickly) but makes more demands;
e) is more responsible;
f) is more questioning;
g) is much better informed.

The learners' handling of individual postmen. They:

a) handle young new entrants firmly but much more sympathetically;
b) know what mix of mail each code-desk operator likes and plan/anticipate to provide it;
c) know how to treat each postman to get the best out of them.

The learners' team-building activities. They:

a) are briefing their teams each week and monitoring day-by-day;
b) have a regular debriefing session with their postmen;
c) are much more aware of throughput hour by hour, dispatch times and mis-sort rates;
d) are setting clearly defined targets.

The learners' awareness of other control areas. They:

a) monitor all those areas that supply them with mail and liaise with their Postal Executives, Level D, (PEs[D]) to ensure a regular supply of the 'right' work (ie, 1st class, 2nd class rebates... appropriate collections);
b) liaise with those areas that receive work from them so that they can plan their flow of traffic to meet their needs;
c) liaise with me about the movement of staff.

The learners' support of their postman and their team. They:

a) provide good 'knowledge of results' to the team as a whole and about each individual's performance;
b) brief their team at the beginning of each shift;
c) make sure that there is always enough work and enough equipment eg, trays, bags, labels, trolleys;
d) make sure all paperwork is available and up to date (eg, work plans, dispatch book, train/platform cards, etc).

The learners' innovative activity and suggestions for improvement. They:

a) are 'thinking on their feet' and making detailed improvements to working methods;
b) have lots of ideas but are careful to discuss them with colleagues and thoroughly work them through before making formal 'suggestions', but then persist in having it properly considered and evaluated.

Overall comment

The SOL coaches seem to be the best informed people in the office. Lots of them have been promoted back into higher grade managerial operational jobs.

Results valued against organisational objectives

It is often difficult to obtain objective measures of a manager's performance. Much work had to be done to provide valid 'knowledge of results' in real time. When this was achieved in our trial office, improved 'capacity for learning' of the managers was quickly demonstrated. In addition to improved individual performance figures, the office performance also improved.

Implications: the prospects for learning organisations

Self Organised Learning offers a new science of human learning; its methods and techniques, including the PLC, have been developed at the CSHL from over 20 years of action research.

In a world of change, Self Organised Learning promotes the development of a personal epistemology of knowledge and skills which enable people to enhance their competences. The Self Organised Learning approach has profound consequences for training policy, for the ways in which expert systems are used, and for management development. It can open up a new vista for open learning practitioners.

In today's climate of intense competition and uncertainty, the skills and knowledge of today are fast becoming the chains of tomorrow's mind. Our evolution towards a more compassionate and efficient future depends on our capacity for learning. It is learning which determines our prospects for survival and our personal and organisational growth.

Chapter Twenty-one

Custom-built Learning Contracts for Corporate Clients

Don Currie

Like most higher education institutions, we at the Southampton Institute have been promulgating the advantages of learning contracts to students and their employer-sponsors for several years and have attempted a variety of approaches to incorporating them as main features of our courses. Until recently, we claimed only a limited degree of success.

In 1991, the Southampton Institute and Southern Water Services Ltd established a Partnership Agreement, which is a contract in which the company sponsors a Fellowship in the Institute's Management Centre. What we might call the 'superior' learning contract is between the two corporate entities. The two organisations are committed to learning from each other. This means that by communicating with each other about matters of mutual interest, the two organisations can exchange views, compare policy on specific issues and collaborate over the solutions to management problems. There is a Partnership Advisory Committee (PAC), made up of an equal number of members from both sides, and a Fellowship Appointments Panel, which is similarly constituted. The PAC meets regularly to discuss current issues and to advise the Fellow on how he or she might best achieve his or her objectives.

The Fellow is responsible for maintaining the relationship between the two parties, although the principal directors of both organisations are members of the Committees, which is an indication of the importance that is attributed to the arrangement. The Partnership Agreement is a written contract and the sponsorship is a financial one.

The Fellow is also responsible for the development of Post-Experience Certificates, Post Graduate Diplomas and Masters-level award-bearing modules; delivering lectures, organising conferences, workshops, short seminars and courses, publishing learned articles, carrying out research and consultancy work and advising on staff and management development in the company.

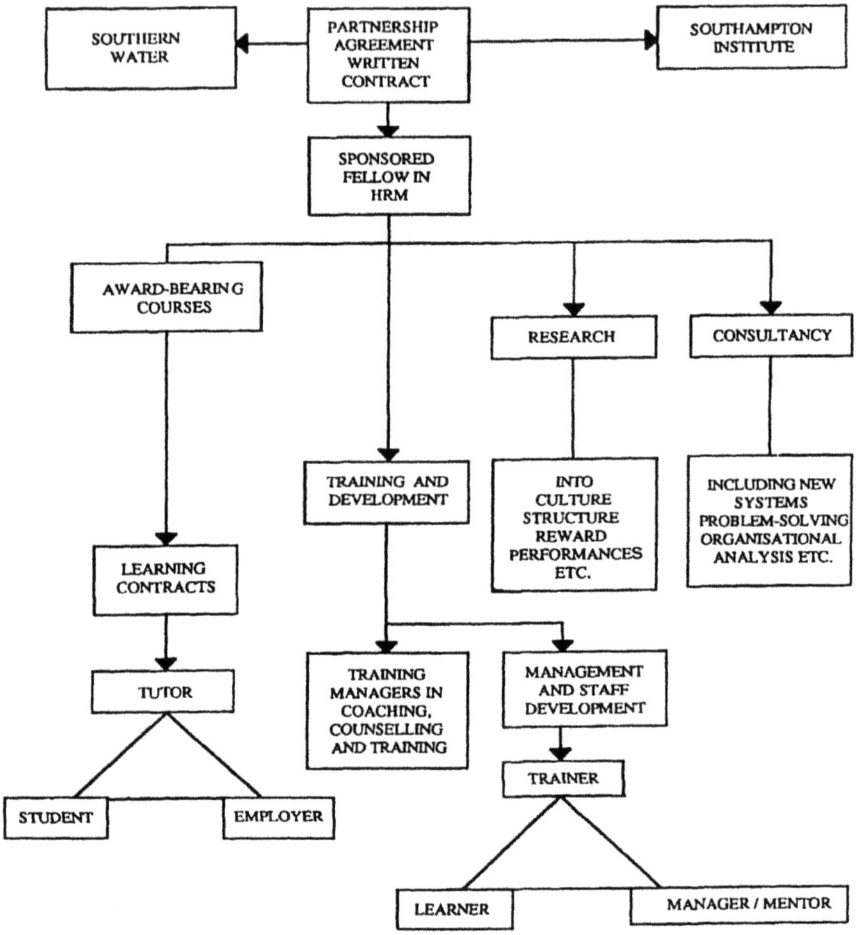

Figure 21.1 *Multi-learning contracts*

This work has been divided into four main activities:

a) award-bearing courses;
b) consultancy;
c) research;
d) in-house training and development.

Figure 21.1 shows the nature of the activities that stem from the main contract. Obviously, the tripartite learning contracts, as they are described above, occur within the 'Award-bearing Courses' branch, but there are others.

Within the 'Training and Development' branch we can see that managers are being trained in coaching, counselling and training. This is being done so that managers can develop their staff effectively. But the managers are not trained solely through the conventional medium of the short course. There is a learning contract between the tutor, the manager and his or her manager.

The tutor will visit the learning manager in his or her work situation and they will spend say, one and a half hours together. The tutor observes the learner at work and coaches and counsels him or her on the job. The manager's manager and the tutor frequently discuss the learner's progress and there are similar discussions between the learner and his/her manager, (who adopts the role of the mentor) in addition to the normal appraisal sessions.

Turning again to Figure 21.1, it can be seen that there are also learning contracts within the 'Management Development' and 'Staff Development' sub-branches. These, of course, are longer-term contracts and the coaching and counselling tend to prepare people for upward progression, as well as to improve their performance in the current roles. In this kind of learning contract, the learner, the manager/mentor and the tutor, all agree upon a developmental plan for the individual. Often, training is added to fill in any significant gaps in the learner's understanding and it is proposed that in future, the Assessment of Prior Learning (APL) will be used to help the learner on towards obtaining qualifications relating to his or her achievements. This decision was reached when the similarity was noticed between the initial meetings to discuss individual plans and the first two stages of APL.

Such contracts exist all over the company from supervisory level upwards. At present, there are about 29 learning contracts in existence in that particular company and this is expected to increase markedly within the next year. A recently completed training needs analysis within the company indicates that there is a need to introduce a considerable amount of new training and development for all staff and a fresh training and development plan will be introduced, bringing with it several variations on the conventional learning contract.

This is not to say that one needs to strike up a relationship as close as one involving financial sponsorship, nor even as close as the relationship described above, in order to achieve the kind of commitment to the learning contract that has arisen in this case. But it does seem to be a good idea to select a single client and set up a dialogue about the advantages of educating, training and developing staff. In this way, the training and development profile is raised within the organisation and its policy on training and development, including the importance of learning contracts, becomes known within the organisation and when that happens, the student-employee's commitment soars. Once the right relationship has been established and consolidated, the word spreads and others begin to show an interest. Having got this far, we are now talking to other organisations about similar arrangements.

Chapter Twenty-two

Institutional Issues in the Implementation of Work-based Learning Contracts

Christopher Harris

A cohort of individual agreements

In addition to the use of learning agreements within formalised undergraduate or postgraduate programmes, Anglia Polytechnic University has recognised the need to facilitate learning by full-time employees in the work place for the furtherance of their professional or career development while causing the minimum disruption to their normal work. Because all the University's course schemes are credit-based, these learning agreements must also allow for credit-accumulation. Evidence of successful completion of the learning outcomes permits the award of academic credit which can be sanctioned either as a Certificate of Credit for the learning achieved or as a named award. The award, from a learning agreement outside an undergraduate or postgraduate course scheme, is made through the institution's Credit Accumulation and Transfer Scheme (CATS), the Open Course Scheme, which is validated to approve any of the University's named awards resulting from an individualised or negotiated programme of study.

Approval for a learning agreement is sought through a formal proposal submitted to a central Approvals Board, a term designed to distinguish this process from validation, which allows for a rapid response to proposals for novel learning arrangements. The approvals process recognises the concept of an enabling learning agreement, a mechanism which gives the necessary framework to a learning agreement, and within which a number of individual learning agreements can subsequently be ratified. Thus the staff, administrative, and committee time needed to develop, propose, and approve an enabling agreement can more rationally be justified since it leads directly to the sanctioning of individual agreements which do not then need to be separately negotiated, proposed, debated, and sanctioned.

The initiative for the enabling learning agreement typically comes from an external organisation or company which has identified a specific learning need for a more or less homogeneous group of employees, members or associates. The approach to the University may be a request for a greater or lesser input of teaching expertise into a learning programme to complement that already envisaged by the organisation. Thus, in this form, the debate about content and teaching/learning strategies takes place with the sponsoring organisation rather than with each participating individual. Alternatively, the request to the University may be solely to place the organisation's own fully planned and resourced in-house programme of learning within the quality assured framework of a learning agreement which would allow the employees/participants to gain formal academic credit for learning achieved, leading eventually to a formal academic award.

The enabling learning agreement submitted for approval will always identify and justify, for example, learning activities/inputs, learning outcomes, forms of assessment, pace and style of learning, mentoring and company support, while also framing parameters within which some of these may vary by individual agreement or negotiation. Thus, using a common approach to a relatively homogeneous group of learners can permit the concluding of a number of individual learning agreements which still allow the individuals, should they wish, to tailor significant aspects of their learning.

Recently, a proposal was made to Anglia's Approvals Board for an enabling learning agreement which related to a group of full-time professionals employed by a local authority, where the proposed agreement identified the following variants which participants could make use of, if they felt they were relevant to their personal learning circumstances:

a) Extended Timescale. Because it was recognised that many of the participants would be professionals working in an area of high demands and because many were likely to be female with additional domestic pressures, the enabling agreement allowed, if necessary, for a very special degree of flexibility in the time-frame of the agreement;

b) Prior Learning. Because it was recognised that the experience level of the participants would be varied it was acknowledged at the outset that some participants might feel they had already achieved aspects of the specified learning and might wish to save time by not repeating the formal learning process. However, they might nevertheless lack formal evidence of that learning, and consequently the enabling agreement allowed for these individuals to opt solely for the specified form of assessment designed to evidence that aspect of their learning;

c) Prior Evidence. Others, however, might judge that they had achieved the learning and also had accumulated adequate, tangible evidence of that learning. The enabling agreement, therefore, allowed these participants to opt out of both the learning activities and the specified assessment and to negotiate on the acceptability for assessment of evidence already available.

Such decisions are explicitly the responsibility of the participant, but none of this precludes renegotiation at a later stage if personal, professional or learning circumstances should demand it.

The emergence of the individual

All individual participants in a work-based learning agreement receive a personalised copy of the individual agreement, and copies are also held by the employer and the University liaison staff nominated to act as the formal link between the individualised learning process and the University as supporting and awarding body. Personal details are gathered from individuals, ideally within a group briefing session, on the procedures and practices of the learning agreement, before this is processed, signed and agreed by all parties: learner, employer, and University. The final stage of the approvals process is a re-submission to the Approvals Board for formal ratification by the Board of the terms and conditions of the group individual agreements.

Vital to this individualisation process is the negotiation by each individual of the specific commitment by their employer to supporting the learning process. This support has two aspects:

a) the employing organisation nominates a company-based mentor to offer informal support, counselling and guidance as 'the critical friend' of the participant;
b) the employing organisation commits itself to practical, material aid in support of the learner.

Where possible the implications and the importance of this company support system is explained face-to-face both to participants and their employers. However, where the agreement deals with employers and participants spread throughout the country or even the near continent, it may only be possible to communicate via detailed briefing papers.

Skills of negotiation

It is at this organisational stage that one must recognise that relying on the individual participant to negotiate aspects of his or her own learning and learning support, however vital to the concept of the learning agreement, is a potentially flawed process. Ultimately the level of satisfaction that results from the negotiation of, for example, the company mentoring or material support, depends almost entirely on the ability and willingness of the participant to negotiate and the willingness of the employer to enter into negotiation.

The Approvals Board, which sanctions the establishment of the enabling agreement and subsequently ratifies the individual learning agreement, will be asked as part of the original proposal document to approve specific company support. Although briefing papers, given both to participant and employer, identify best practice for mentoring and best models for material support, it is ultimately not possible and, in the spirit of a learning agreement arguably not desirable, for the University to operate an interventionist control over the participant's individual negotiation process.

A recent example of individually negotiated company support in a group of individual learning agreements showed a range of company material support. Many of the concluded negotiations had resulted in finalised company support very close to what had been exemplified as normal practice, but at either extreme of the range fell the following two examples:

a) Participant A: Company Support
   - modification of formal working hours;
   - access to industrial archives;
   - appropriate clerical support;
   - reasonable use of communications equipment.
b) Participant B: Company Support
   - reimbursement of necessary travelling costs.

Thus the Approvals Board may feel itself left with the dilemma of whether or not to ratify the individual learning agreement of Participant B with this minimal support. The Board could refuse to ratify the individual agreement because of the employer's apparent unwillingness further to support the employee's learning process. However, it may be that the employer is truly unable to allow further time, staff or financial support for the employee's learning process. Moreover, it may be that the employee accepts this minimal level of support in preference to being unable to benefit from participating in the agreement. This is, finally, the personal negotiating decision of the individual participant, and it is wholly in the spirit of the learning agreement that this participant should accept this responsibility for the conditions and terms of his or her learning.

An art not a science: but a valuable one!

Currently a supportive exchange of letters is taking place with this participant to establish which of these interpretations is the case, but whatever processes are put in place for the creation, administration, quality control and support for an individual learning agreement, I do not believe that this type of hard decision can be or indeed should be circumvented by intervention from the University. I do believe that the strength of the individual learning agreement lies in these very personal, learner-centred decisions. That *individual learners are facilitated in undertaking learning* which is directly relevant to their personal or professional needs, and that this process is founded on mutual *agreement* between all those parties who have the power to support the process, encompasses all that is positive and exciting about the use of this mechanism in higher education.

Part Three:

The Future

Chapter Twenty-three

The Place and Potential Use of Learning Contracts in Higher Education

Mike Laycock and John Stephenson

A Brief Review of Practice

An era of change

Higher education in the UK is facing a critical era in its evolution. Perhaps the most important ingredient in the miscellany of changes is the recognition of the need for change itself. Central to that recognition is the necessity of creating a system which:

a) acknowledges a shared responsibility for learning between teacher and learner;
b) concentrates on educational processes as well as educational outcomes;
c) can franchise and accredit off-campus learning; and
d) is responsive to the individual learning needs of an increasing, diverse student intake where didactic teaching is giving way to increased learning facilitation.

Whether the recognition of these directions of change derives primarily from ideological preference or from economic necessity will, no doubt, form the background to future debate. Our task as educators, however, is to ensure that quality of the student experience is enhanced and not diminished by change, whatever its impetus. From the evidence at the conference and the chapters in this book, it should be obvious that our contributors have recognised the value of learning contracts in implementing many of the ideas central to the current changes in higher education.

Commonality of approach

From all the contributors, some common approaches have been identified. They have emphasised the importance of:

a) enabling a shared responsibility for negotiating goals or objectives;
b) recognising that the process issues of planning, monitoring and review of educational outcomes are as important as the outcomes themselves;
c) involving the major 'stakeholders' (students, staff, external examiners, employers/mentors, employees) in the processes of managing off-campus learning; and
d) the need for staff and students to recognise and understand the shift in roles and responsibilities that use of learning contracts implies.

Variability of practice

While some commonality of approach can be identified, so too can the variability of practice. Thus far the use of learning contracts is evident in:

a) components within traditional degree programmes such as project work, placement, seminars;
b) activities aimed at developing specific skills;
c) the assessment or self-assessment of learning outcomes or competences; and
d) whole educational programmes.

The variety of practice in the use of learning contracts can be accommodated within two interlocking continua (Figure 23.1) related to primary focus and context. The *primary learning focus* can be the learning which derives from the *process* of contracting or the learning *outcomes* from the studies themselves. Process-oriented contracts are concerned with the means by which learners can be empowered to have more active control over their own learning experience by setting goals, identifying and responding to problems and monitoring progress. Outcome-oriented contracts are related to the content mastered and the experiences gained or with accreditation of work-based learning and, in the case of independent study, to the accreditation of whole programmes of study. The *context* continuum ranges from small activities within individual classes to students' whole programmes of study.

The characteristics of contracts within the four quadrants in Figure 23.1 can be summarised as follows:

Quadrant 1: outcomes – part of programme

Some contributors have identified the use of learning contracts in earning academic credit towards part of a degree programme. Typically, this approach is in evidence where some form of work-based learning requires accreditation (see for example, Hodgson, Chapter 14 and Marshall and Mill, Chapter 15).

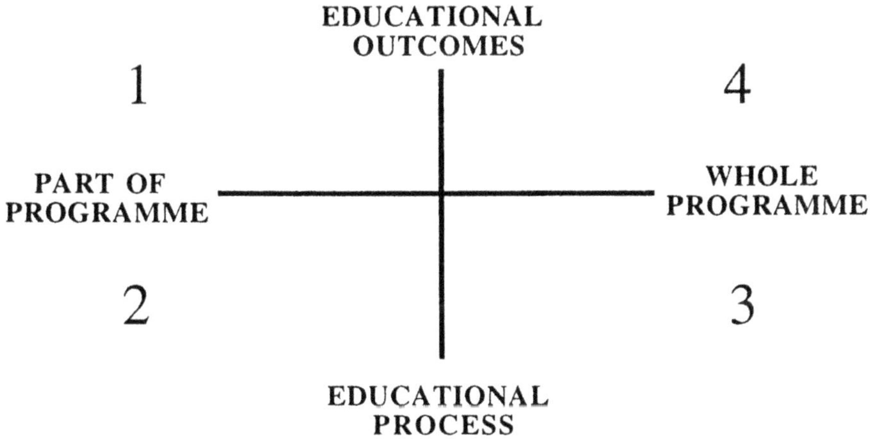

Figure 23.1 *The current use of learning contracts: the primary focus-context grid*

Quadrant 2: process – part of programme

Where contributors have highlighted the importance of learning contracts in supporting process issues for a part of the academic programme, their use is typically related to skills development or in support of aspects of educational organisation, such as seminars (see for example, Gosling, Chapter 6, and Binns, Chapter 7).

Quadrant 3: process – whole programme

The distinction between process and outcome issues is less clear where learning contracts are used for whole educational programmes. Nevertheless, contributors such as Kathy Moore (Chapter 18) have stressed the use of learning contracts in supporting the process of 'self-managed learning', in her case for the MBA Programme at Roffey Park; 'the learning contract is ... about getting learners to think about the process of learning itself'.

Quadrant 4: outcomes – whole programme

Where learning contracts are intimately associated with the accredited outcomes of whole educational programmes, contributors have concentrated more on identifying the institutional procedures governing the approval of learning contracts and the assessment of their outcomes (see for example Piper and Wilson, Chapter 4, and O'Reilly, Chapter 5).

Issues Raised by the Use of Learning Contracts

Most of the issues raised by the examples presented in Part Two are found in the areas of:

a) managing a process which quite clearly responds to individual needs and interests;

b) resolving the extant demands of the course with the 'negotiability' of contract learning;
c) attempting to operate within an institutional system that is culturally at variance with that implied by the use of learning contracts.

Managing scarce resources in response to individual needs

One common issue to emerge from the examples is that responding to every individual need – as implied by some learning contract approaches – can be resource-intensive. This is particularly important at the present time, given the pressure to maintain standards in the context of expanding student numbers and a declining unit of resource.

The drive towards the expansion of student intake without commensurate increases in staffing has already prompted HEIs to think of ways in which teaching and learning methods must change towards enabling students to be more autonomous learners. The implementation of Credit Accumulation and Transfer Schemes (CATS), the development of approaches like the Assessment of Prior and Prior Experiential Learning (APL/APEL) to manage varying levels of intake and the move towards accelerated degree programmes, all point to a system which is becoming increasingly customer-oriented. At the same time there is also the recognition that the increased intake will exhibit a much greater diversity of background in terms of prior qualifications, age, ethnic origin and social status thus exacerbating the problem of marshalling resources in response to student need.

The irony of expansion is that responsiveness to the student as customer appears to imply a responsiveness which is being perceived as resource-intensive. If properly managed, learning contracts need not be so. Indeed, there are a number of ways in which they can make more effective use of scarce resources. Resource-intensity is often associated with attempts to introduce contracts within a management structure geared towards more traditional modes of delivery. The resource advantages of switching from teacher- to student-managed learning will accrue if ways can be found of making the institutional infrastructure correspond with the cultural imperatives of autonomous learning. The move towards learner responsibility and autonomy suggests a resource shift from teacher to learner. Students, rather than staff, will increasingly be expected to *manage* learning, perhaps using materials delivered more efficiently via carefully crafted packages through what in effect might be 'paper modules', provided some of the staff resources released from the routine oral delivery of information can be diverted to servicing the support structures for the process of students' learning from such materials.

A timetabling solution

The management infrastructure needs to be consistent with the varying cycles of student activity involved in contracting. Traditional didactic teaching can be accommodated in regular doses of fixed and pre-determined student-staff contact, usually calculated on hourly-based weekly-accounted timetables. Our contributors have identified a different and more varied distribution of contact needs, with *two* periods of intensive activity – the preparation of plans and the assessment of achievement – interspersed with periods of intense student activity which is less dependent upon tutor contact.

One of the two intensive activities, assessment, is also intensive on traditional courses. Most students are individually assessed and the structure of the academic timetable accounts for this. It is the earlier peak of activity which attracts most concern since the traditional timetable does not, at least on an institutional basis, account for a period of negotiating and approving educational plans. Learning contracts imply a cyclical process of learning of the kind described by Kolb and his associates (Kolb *et al.*, 1974) which can be redefined (as identified by O'Reilly, Chapter 5) as a *plan, do and review* cycle. Though the planning and review/assessment periods might be resource-intensive, the doing/monitoring period might require less contact if students were enabled to manage their own learning. A learning contract would, in part, support that management. It would not be impossible to create an institutional infrastructure which supported, say, an 'annual' or 'semesterised' learning cycle with appropriate procedures (of the kind described by, for example, Piper and Wilson, Chapter 4) to formalise the process. Attempting to fit the approach within traditional structures means, for example, that traditional weekly notions of contact-time are impinging negatively on the process. A switch from hourly-based, weekly-accounted staff management to case-load annual timetabling would a) recognise the peaks and troughs in tutoring student-managed learning, leaving staff with alternating busy and fallow periods consistent with the distinctive sequence of varying student needs which student managed learning implies and b) would suggest a totally different perspective from which to judge the issue of resource-intensiveness.

Availability of external resources

Contributors have also pointed to the way in which HEIs can utilise and share resources in the community. In the case of learning contracts with employees (eg, Robertson, Chapter 16 and Harris, Chapter 22) the workplace can be used as a resource for learning. The use of mentors (eg, Drew and Lawson, Chapter 8, Hodgson, Chapter 14, and Brockbank, Chapter 17) in the shared facilitation and assessment of learning has also been identified.

The participation pay off

With a switch from traditional methods of transmission to open/distance learning methods and materials, from the traditional timetable of lectures, seminars and tutorials to more group-based activity, from teachers being the source of information to student-managed learning in libraries, workshops and the workplace, and the involvement of others such as employers in the learning process, it is conceivable that one 'participation pay off' may be a *less* intensive 'teaching load'. Certainly there are greater opportunities for critical dialogue. With regular contexts for monitoring and offering feedback on student progress, coupled with more devices to assist self-monitoring and self-assessment (learning contracts, profiles, records of achievement), the facilitation of learning may become more resource-efficient.

Course demands and student negotiation

Contributors have consistently referred to the importance of learning contracts in increasing student ownership of what is learnt and that the degree of ownership is positively linked to the achievement of goals. Many have referred to the process of negotiation as central to the acquisition of ownership. Yet in most cases, staff are attempting to fit contract learning into an educational culture which has extant demands, where course objectives, content, timing and location are set by the institution. It should not be surprising, therefore, that contributors such as Spaull, Chapter 10, and Hay-Smith, Chapter 13, have identified a potential lack of understanding of the process on the part of stakeholders. Drew and Lawson, Chapter 8, admit that 'the learning contract sits rather uneasily in the whole course structure...given that competences are specified and course work required'. Using learning contracts becomes problematic where the prevailing institutional ethos supports, both culturally and structurally, a more traditional 'non-negotiable' approach to higher education.

McCarthy, Chapter 2, however, has offered aspects of course content and process for which there may be a 'range of negotiability'. Piper and Wilson, Chapter 4, O'Reilly, Chapter 5, and Harris, Chapter 22, have all indicated how, while developing specific criteria for the approval and assessment of the outcomes of contracts, alternative but equally institutionally valid course procedures such as Registration or Approvals Boards can themselves become the extant requirements for quality assurance and the maintenance of academic standards.

Institutional disjunction and the purpose of higher education

In the main, the examples offered by contributors focus attention on the implementation of a process which is culturally at variance with the prevailing hegemony. There is a disjunction between institution-centred demands and the student-centredness of contract learning. The wider debate that the use of learning contracts implies is that which concerns the purpose of an HE institution: *is the institution's role one of 'Director of Learning' or one of a 'Resource for Learning'?*

The *Institution as Director* of learning perpetuates implicit and explicit assumptions of the learning process as being owned and controlled by the institution, servicing the demands of the course and the needs and interests of staff. The institution as director of learning derives its legitimacy from 'external' control over objectives, content, timing, pace, location and forms of assessment. Once choice of study, or in the case of modularised programmes,

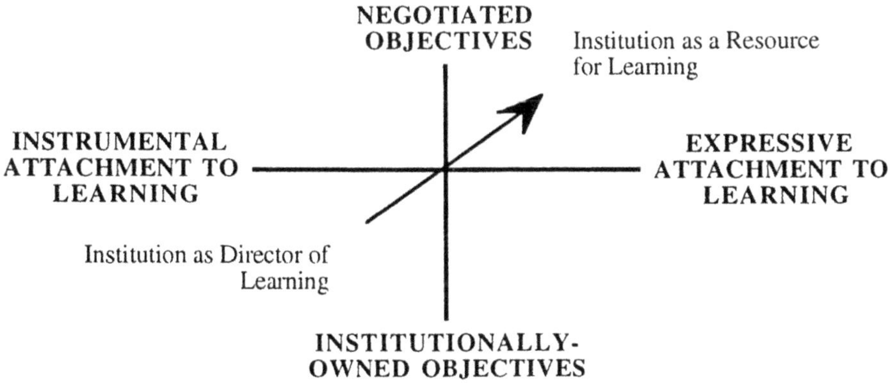

Figure 23.2 *Using learning contracts in the shift from an institution as 'director of learning' to a 'resource for learning'*

choice of combinations of study, has been made, student control over the process is largely abandoned. Little investment, by students, in the means by which learning is accomplished is permissable within this model, although, no doubt, there is a positive attachment to the ends or outcome of the process – the award. Students may be said to have an instrumental attachment to the process of learning and a passive, dependent role in that process.

The *Institution as a Resource* for learning, by contrast, would use its human and physical resources to support the learning needs of students and other stakeholders. Its purpose is cooperative, promoting a dialectical rather than didactic learning process, a shift from dependent to autonomous study, from transmission to interpretation, from the authoritarian to the democratic. The student is encouraged, in negotiation, to develop greater ownership of the objectives, content, procedures and processes of learning. Greater attachment to both the means and ends of the learning process is thus made possible for the student. The institution may be said to be encouraging a more expressive attachment to the process of learning and a more active, independent role for the student.

It is in the shift from the institution as 'Director of Learning' to the institution as a 'Resource for Learning' that the learning contract can increasingly provide the means by which responsibility and accountability in learning can be achieved and where students can demonstrate a greater expressive attachment to learning (see Figure 23.2).

Future uses of learning contracts in higher education

Our discussion of the future use of learning contracts in higher education takes account of some developments already in place, some about to emerge and some which can only be envisioned. Central to the discussion is the notion that, for the use of learning contracts to be embedded in HEIs, both cultural and structural change is necessary. We take as our key issues:

a) learning contracts and modularisation;
b) learning contracts and open/distance learning;
c) the move from traditional teaching methods to tutor groups;
d) learning contracts as an overall strategy for learning;
e) learning contracts and the learning institution.

Learning Contracts and Modularisation

While some contributors (Piper and Wilson, Chapter 4, Nicholls, Chapter 11, and Hay-Smith, Chapter 13) have described the use of learning contracts within particular modular units, few have considered their use for inter-modular integration. It is an aspect of contract learning which requires further consideration.

Learning contracts within individual modules

Many of our contributors have envisioned the wider use of learning contracts (Nicholls, Chapter 11, Stewart-David, Chapter 12, and Hodgson, Chapter 14) on modular courses. Nicholls, in particular, in his description of a course unit at Manchester Metropolitan University suggests that

> The adoption of contracts for all course units would perhaps lead to more thought being devoted both by teachers and students to questions of coherence and progress, to consideration of the respective contributions of different units towards encouraging a wide range of competences, and to explicit attempts to plug gaps in a student's educational experience.

The logic of modularisation presents a strong case for the use of learning contracts within individual modules. 'Mix and match' schemes will mean tutors having to cope with a greater variety of students with a greater variety of experience from different feeder modules and with different intended destination modules. Learning contracts can accommodate these different start and end points, and can enable students to relate their module programmes to their distinctive needs and aspirations, providing a course experience which has, for each student, coherence and overall integrity.

Learning contracts for inter-modular use

The problems of cohort diversity and programme coherence identifiable within individual modules are still more visible on the institutional scale. Modularisation has presented institutions with both opportunities and challenges in offering students much more flexibility in the choice of course provision. Few, if any, have attempted to couple choice of units of study with the idea that students can 'negotiate their own learning programmes' nor instituted a mechanism for achieving this.

All institutions are seeking ways to provide evaluations of prior educational experiences other than conventional entry qualifications and, on the basis of diagnoses, to provide flexible learning experiences for students. There are dangers, however, that in an effort to create more flexibility, modularisation may lead to a fragmented learning framework. The major issue is the extent to which, in recognising the development of cohort diversity, there can be an identifiable outcome integrity. For some, there are real concerns about learning development, progression and, most important of all, the coherent integration of the student's overall learning experience.

Individual learning contracts for overall module integration

For the future, we may consider the creation of a systematic framework which will permit the inter-modular development of an integrated study programme based on the negotiation of learning. Rather than institutionally-determined, it will be created in the form of a democratic partnership between the student, the institution and, where relevant, employers/practitioners. This is not to deny that some core units of study may be non-negotiable. Enabling the student to provide a justification, in terms of their own aims and objectives for learning, for the integration of optional units and other forms of experiential learning would enhance student motivation and ownership of their studies. That partnership should provide procedures and mechanisms which recognise the backgrounds of a diverse student population, their programme plans, a means by which they can monitor progress, and means by which they can review their own learning. The use of a learning contract will be instrumental in this cycle of learning for inter-modular integration (see Figure 23.3 overleaf).

The learning contract cycle is not closed. Its iteration could occur at convenient points in the academic timetable (on a term, semester or level basis). The implication is that the organisational infrastructure will reflect the cyclical process of learning. The creation of a learning contract would imply an institutional 'planning period'.

An Institutional planning period

There are sound reasons for introducing a planning period for all students at the start of an institutional modular scheme. The guiding principles of such a period would include reflections on previous experience, acknowledging present capabilities and justifying the coherence of academic progression. It would represent the means by which staff and students could jointly negotiate the academic enterprise in a more democratic partnership.

For *staff* there would be the opportunity to:

a) explain the relevance of the units offered;
b) establish the importance of 'core' elements regarded as essential to balance, progression and professional requirements of the subject which are non-negotiable;

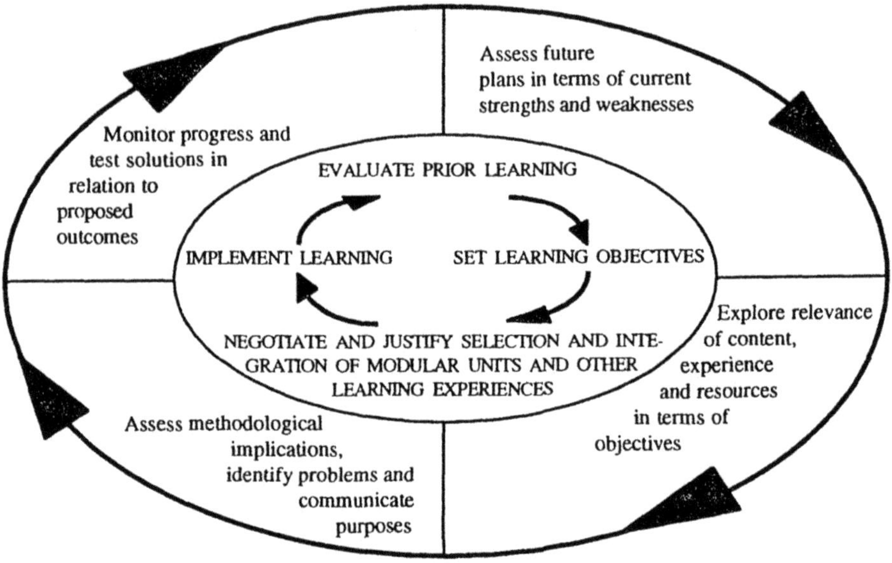

Figure 23.3 *The contract learning cycle and modularisation*

c) assess and accredit prior learning;
d) engage, with students, in a diagnosis of study skills and other personal transferable skills.

For *students* there would be the opportunity to:

a) reflect on prior learning and seek means by which this could be assessed;
b) examine their role/responsibility in higher education;
c) profile present capabilities in skills and knowledge;
d) set learning objectives;
e) with guidance, prepare a learning contract justifying the coherence of their modular programme including negotiable and non-negotiable elements.

An assessment and review period

Having established such a period, institutions may wish to consider a complementary 'assessment and review period' as a completing element in the cycle with suitable systems for monitoring progress in the intervening period. The inclusion of mechanisms, in addition to conventional assessment practices, that encourage self- and peer-assessment could form appropriate adjuncts to both formative and summative assessment.

Embedding such structures into the learning environment implies alternative arrangements to those which currently exist. Many contributors, for example, have indicated alternative institutional structures to support the agreement of learning contracts, systems which permit clarification of the processes involved, and means by which the outcomes of contracts might be assessed.

Among other considerations are the extent to which the planning, monitoring and reviewing processes might be credited, given that many staff might wish to see units of knowledge acquisition as the only legitimate accreditable activity (despite external pressures for the recognition of the development of skills such as planning and organisation), and their resourcing, given pressures towards increasing participation rates in higher education. Moreover, giving credit for the completion of planning, monitoring and review would be just recognition for the valuable learning which students would derive from the processes of planning, monitoring, self-assessment and progress review.

Learning contracts and open/distance learning

It is clear from current developments in higher education that traditional didactic teaching is giving way to more flexible open learning approaches. Certainly, such open learning is seen as providing one answer to increasing student numbers. There are possibilities, for example, for releasing constraints on space, overlapping in unit timetabling, linear development and attendance patterns.

Such a change will, however, demand more resourcefulness on the part of the learner in managing open/distance learning. If open/distance learning releases institutions from some of the management of the learning process, responsibility for the individual management of that process can be enabled by the use of a learning contract. Contract learning could enable students to:

a) manage their own personal timetable;
b) engage intelligently with materials;
c) reflect on the relevance of materials; and
d) review their understanding of materials.

European open/distance learning

We have, as a consequence of the information revolution, ever more powerful means of storing, manipulating and retrieving knowledge which, in the future, will render some of the current approaches to education and training obsolete. Perhaps, more importantly, with the impact of Europe 1993, involving the biggest single market comprising 340 million people, the demand for growth in higher education and the civil rights of citizens for mobility within the European Community will mean creating frameworks that facilitate access, movement and transfer.

An important new report from the Commission on Open and Distance Higher Education in the European Community (Commission of the European Communities, 1992), sets out the political agenda. It describes open distance learning as:

> any form of study not under the continuous or immediate supervision of tutors, but which nevertheless benefits from the planning, guidance and tuition of a tutorial organisation....Because Open Distance Learning is meant to be adaptable to the pace of the student the material is generally structured in units or modules geared to specific learning outcomes.
>
> The presence of a strong autonomous component in Open Distance Learning is very much in keeping with the ideas current in higher education of making students more responsible for attaining their own learning objectives. (p. 6)

In addition to creating opportunities for students in Europe to study distance courses from abroad (where the value of learning contracts has already been noted by Nicholls, Chapter 11, and Stewart-David, Chapter 12), the Report points to potential in linking 'distance teaching institutions with regional training consortia in particular for meeting training needs for local industry' (p. 13) and 'creating trans-European networks for training...' (p. 7). The need for continuing education and training is likely to intensify since, as the Report indicates:

> it is salutary to note that even if useful knowledge has a half-life as long as ten years, intellectual capital is then depreciating at 7%/year (which is a much higher rate than the recruitment of new graduates), with a corresponding reduction in the effectiveness of the work force. (p. 19)

Provision within institutions, therefore, of flexible entry and exit points, where participants can negotiate learning objectives and plan learning programmes of particular professional relevance, will increasingly characterise higher education in the future. The function of learning contracts to enable that process will be invaluable.

The tutorial organisation

Our vision of the use of learning contracts in the university of the future has one final component. We have noted the importance of planning, monitoring and review periods in the institutional cycle of learning. For the process to find a supportive contextual home, the current organisation of teaching (lectures, seminars, tutorials) will require some adaptation, particularly when associated with open or distance learning. The Commission states:

> Distance higher education is faced with the paradox that the requirement of physical attendance in order to receive tutoring and guidance would seem to violate the principle of freedom of time and place which is the hallmark of distance education. On the other hand student support services constitute an indispensable complement to packaged materials in order to ensure feedback and inter-activity. (p. 31)

Reorganisation of the structure of student support is equally important for college-based learning. What is required is a tutorial organisation which can cope with large numbers of students and which will provide the context for feedback and inter-activity and be the institutional locus for the use of learning contracts, profiling, portfolio development, personal transferable skills development and other current innovations. In return, the development and management of learning contracts will provide a framework for constructive dialogue between students and students and between students and staff on each student's progress.

We might offer the notion of a tutor group system in place of the college-based lecture programme and in support of a resource-based system providing support for:

a) *contract development and management*, which would include the provision of a consistent 'home base' for students throughout the life of their programme, supporting students in the negotiation of learning contracts, engaging in critical dialogue for reviewing the progress of learning through profiling/portfolio development;
b) *personal transferable skills development*, enabling it to be integrated within course delivery, developed in the main through active learning situations (workshops, games, simulations, etc.) rather than through open learning materials;
c) *experiential learning*, providing opportunity for developing a shared clarity of purpose amongst different participants including employers, a focus for the process of negotiation between student, institution and employer and the review of progress from client-based project work, work experience and placement.

There is no reason, of course, to view these tutor groups as mutually exclusive. Staff development would ultimately determine the extent to which appropriate skills in facilitation would enable all functions to be incorporated in one form of group.

Learning contracts as a universal strategy for learning?

Between them, our contributors present a catalogue of the different ways and contexts in which learning contracts are able to develop different aspects of student capability. It is our view that the essential feature of the learning contract which enables this to happen is the obligation it places on students to be *accountable* as well as responsible for their own learning. Learning contracts have to be negotiated and justified at their outset and demonstrated and reviewed at their completion. Each of these activities involves dialogue – with other students, tutors and the relevant academic and/or vocational 'field'. Not only does this dialogue develop useful personal skills and qualities, it also extends students' understanding of the effectiveness and relevance of their own learning. Programmes of study which allow students to receive and regurgitate information – whether passively or actively – can easily allow students to avoid addressing these issues. A well-managed learning contract approach, with suitable tutorial support for students, ensures that students own and understand as well as merely cover the content of their programmes. It focuses on the development of the student's overall capability – the ability to be responsible and accountable for their own continuing personal and professional development.

Learning contracts can be used for small-scale activities as well as whole student programmes (Figure 23.1). They can also be used for a succession of small-scale activities within a negotiated contract covering a whole programme. Learning contracts are appropriate for students at any level because they make the student's starting point the basis for the student's programme, and for any aspiration – whether academic, personal or vocational. By taking students from their starting levels towards their aspirations, learning contracts focus on students making progress in their chosen field. They are suitable for any level and for a wider variety of learning locations than is normally provided within the classroom. It could be argued that they have a universal application.

An approach to education which develops students' personal qualities and skills, promotes understanding of key concepts and the relevance of what is learned, focuses on helping students take themselves forward and is almost universally applicable, deserves serious consideration. Students reared on receptive learning may not readily take to it, be convinced of its merits or, more significantly, may lack the confidence to commit themselves to being responsible for their programmes. If students complete a succession of contracts, beginning with small-scale or easily manageable activities and each one builds on the experience of its predecessors, student sophistication in both the process and content of their contracts will be enhanced.

In Figure 23.4, we bring all of the aforementioned together and show how a succession of student negotiated contracts can lead to student sophistication in a range of high level skills within the context of the student's specialised field of academic and/or vocational interest. The Learning Contract Capability Spiral begins with the student's existing level of capability and progresses through five activities, each of which enables students to develop different aspects of their capability.

With each successive contract, students become more sophisticated in each activity, and are able to progress their studies in more complex situations and with a greater depth of understanding. The succession of contracts represents a spiral of escalating student capability and student commitment as their sense of ownership of the direction of study is integrated with feelings of power derived from achievement legitimately attributable to their own efforts and initiative.

Learning contracts and the learning institution

We envisage the possibility of creating an institutional framework which supports a learning process based on successive student experiences of

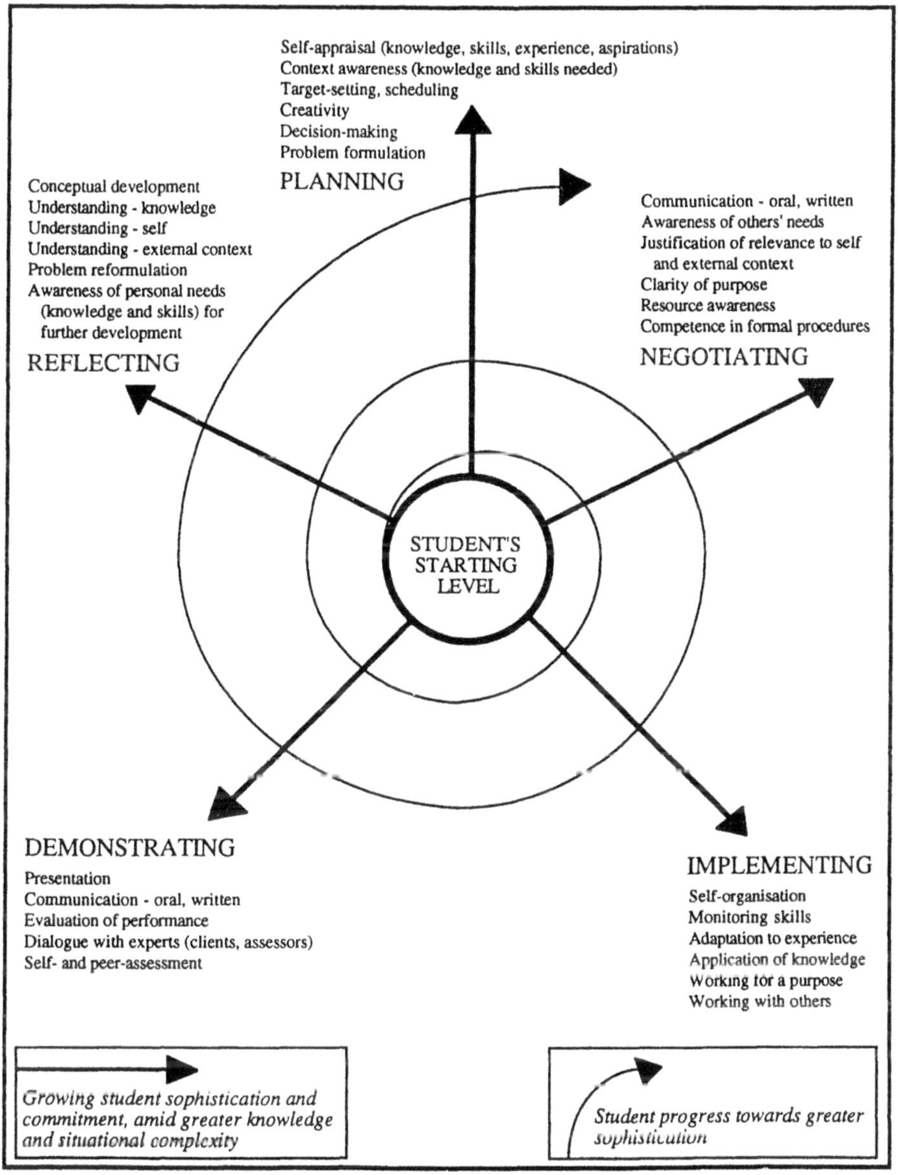

Figure 23.4 *The learning contracts capability spiral*

planning, negotiating, monitoring and demonstrating and reflecting on their own learning – whether on independent study programmes, modular schemes, using open learning materials or learning from a variety of work-based experiences. At the heart of this iterative process based on the construction and revision of learning contracts is the vision of an institution which is a resource for learning – a learning institution where participants, including school leavers, those returning to learn and those seeking professional updating can jointly negotiate their higher education programme by entering and exiting at points which equate to their accredited learning.

The learning institution will provide students with:

a) support for lifelong learning;
b) access to expertise;
c) access to specialist resources;
d) opportunities for dialogue and peer support;
e) quality assurance and accreditation.

The learning contract, as a core enabling device in the learning institution will ensure:

a) a means of providing rigour, public credibility and accountability;
b) a means of maximising access and responding to an increasing and increasingly varied intake;
c) a means of negotiating access to resources and expertise; and
d) the creation of a cooperative, lifelong learning framework.

Such a scenario requires cultural and structural change in higher education. It challenges the traditional role of higher education as the controller of what students learn and of the intellectual capital of the nation in favour of one in which higher education institutions are as open to user needs as public libraries, providing expertise, specialist resources, quality assurance and tutorial support for learners of all kinds taking responsibility and being accountable for their own learning. Radical change is coming. Given the combined efforts of a number of pioneering academic staff in institutions throughout the UK, some of whom have contributed to this book, we are certain that the learning contract will play its part in this major paradigm shift.

References

Commission of the European Communities (1992) Open Distance Learning in European Community, Brussels.

Kolb, DA, Rubin, IM and McIntyre, JM (1974) *Organisational Psychology: An experimental approach to organizational behaviour*, New Jersey: Prentice Hall.

Index

For Product Safety Concerns and Information please contact our EU representative GPSR@taylorandfrancis.com
Taylor & Francis Verlag GmbH, Kaufingerstraße 24, 80331 München, Germany

www.ingramcontent.com/pod-product-compliance
Ingram Content Group UK Ltd.
Pitfield, Milton Keynes, MK11 3LW, UK
UKHW020205200926
475702UK00004B/628

* 9 7 8 1 1 3 8 1 6 3 3 5 5 *